SUNBURST

A Generational Anthology of Education,
Marriage, Love, Integrity, and Family.

FRANCES LOWE

KP PUBLISHING COMPANY

ISBN: 978-1-950936-74-8 (Paperback)
ISBN: 978-1-950936-75-5 (eBook)
Library of Congress Control Number: 2022906021

Editor: KP Publishing Editorial Services
Proofreader: Frank Williams
Cover Design: Juan Roberts
Interior Design: Jennifer Houle
Literary Director: Sandra L. James

Published by:

KP Publishing Company
Publisher of Fiction, Nonfiction & Children's Books
Valencia, CA 91355
www.kp-pub.com

Printed in the United States of America

DEDICATION

I dedicate this book to my parents,
Mr. Robert Gorley, Sr., and Mrs. Elizabeth Nash Gorley.

INTRODUCTION

Sunburst is one of the most unique books you will ever read. This book spans over seven decades of history. The nineteen stories written in this book are based on real-life occurrences.

Sunburst will be enjoyed by all readers, from pre-teen upward. It is a book for all cultures and ethnic groups, not primarily an African American experience. *Sunburst* began as a simple project. My great-nephew, Ezekiel Joubert III, PhD., who is an educator and scholar, interested in the African American experience, asked me to write something about the people who inspired me to pass on to the next generations. Ezekiel also asked other senior family members, friends, co-workers, and others to leave a written legacy for the next generations, whether the writings are published or not published.

In June 2020, some family members and friends of various ages had a very lively discussion on how to better cope with many of the world's current problems. The ages ranged from sixteen to ninety. As I mentioned, it was lively; however, everyone agreed that education is the one thing in life that the entire world needs to avoid many life problems and solve some of the issues we are facing today. For example, we are still in the COVID-19 pandemic, and many people do not understand why we should be vaccinated, wear masks, wash our hands, and keep a social distance.

Sunburst addresses many topics: education, marriage, love, integrity, history, difficult lessons, believing what children say, hospitality, the Great Migration, and much more. In some stories, readers will form their own conclusion, as with ***A Tale of Three Wives***. I hope readers will learn something from each story, be enlightened, empowered, educated, inspired, and excel in new and exciting knowledge.

CONTENTS

MY HOME TOWN
EATONTON, GEORGIA

Eatonton is a city in and county seat of Putnam County, Georgia.

Eatonton is located close to the center of Georgia between Putnam and Jasper Counties. It was named after William Eaton, an officer and diplomat involved in the First Barbary War. Eatonton is 63.7 miles from Hartsfield-Jackson Atlanta Airport. It has 20.51 square miles (about twice the area of JFK Airport) of land area and 0.10 square miles of water area.

Population: 6,986

Demographics:

Black or African American	57.8%
White	39.9%
Other	1.76%
Two or more races	0.33%
Asian	0.23%

Interesting Sites:
Crooked Pines Farm
Georgia Writers Museum
Historic Uncle Remus Museum
Rock Eagle Mound
Rock Hawk Effigy and Trails
The Plaza Arts Center

Home of Significant Celebrated People from Eatonton

Sarah Gorley Abrams- First African American City Clerk of
  Eatonton (2000)

Merrell Bennekin, African American Attorney

Marcia Bennekin-Woodham, African American Attorney/ Federal Judge

Harrison Cobb – African American Business Owner and Casket Builder

Andy Corley – Co-founder, CEO, Chairman, and President of
  Eyeonics, Inc.

Salonia Daniels –African American Brick mason, Barber Shop and
  Restaurant Owner

David C. Driskell – African American Artist, leading Scholar, and
  Curator

Roberta Franklin –African American Owner of "Miss Roberta's Café
  in Five Point

Vincent Hancock, Three-time Olympic Gold Medalist, Skeet Shooter

Joel Chandler Harris, Author of the Children's Fables of Uncle Remus

Hiram E. Little Sr., Tuskegee Airman

Leonard Little – Medical Doctor

Jack Montgomery – Owner of Fish Market, The Montgomery
  Homes, named in his honor

Hardy Pennamon - African American Pharmacist – (Before integration)

John Reid – First African American Mayor (2002) of Eatonton

Rubin Sanders and Raymond Simmons – First African American
  Shoe Repair Shop

Cathy Truett, Founder of Chick-fil-A

Alice Walker, Author of The Color Purple, a 1982 novel, winner of
  the 1983 Pulitzer Prize for Fiction, and the National Book Award
  for Fiction, adapted into a film and musical

MY HOME IN EATONTON

A TRIBUTE TO MY PARENTS

My Father
Mr. Robert Gorley, Sr.
United States Army

My Father, Mr. Robert Gorley, Sr. (1986)

My daddy, Mr. Robert Gorley Sr. was born to Ella Presley in 1912 in Atlanta, Georgia. Daddy is the only child of Ella Presley. His father is Andrew McFalls. He never knew his birth father or his mother, as she died as a result from complications of his childbirth. Daddy was taken in by his mother's sister Maggie Presley Gorley and her husband Andrew Gorley, and their six children. He had a deep love and respect for his aunt Maggie, and he loved his foster brothers and sisters.

"Trust in the Lord," was my father's favorite saying, and his sound advice to his children was, "Get some learning; that is why I am sending you to school. Learn to figure, and don't spend every penny you get."

Even though he only had a second-grade education, he was a wise man. In 1936, my dad and mom, Elizabeth, married, and Daddy worked as a janitor at the Eatonton Courthouse. World War II changed our lives as he was drafted into the Army; at the time, they had three children, Robert, Leila, and me. My daddy was 32 years old. His military assignment was a blessing in disguise because he was trained to be a painter and electrician.

He distinguished himself by earning several awards and medals while serving in the United States Army. His medals included: The European-African Middle Eastern Service Medal with a Bronze Star, Asiatic-Pacific Medal, World War II Victory Medal, and a Good Conduct Medal. Among his personal papers is a letter from Harry S. Truman, the 33rd president of the United States.

After returning from the war, he began a life-long career painting houses and doing electrical work. He established himself as a businessman with an excellent reputation of being honest and trustworthy. Daddy became the number one house painter in Eatonton, working for White and Black businesses and families. He was a well-respected mentor who taught many young men how to paint. Some of his students, including his brother, Buster, left Eatonton and obtained well-paying jobs in several other cities. He was among the Black entrepreneurs of his time, as he also did carpentry and became a property owner. In addition, Daddy was a deacon in his church, Ebenezer Baptist Church, where he served as a group leader for many years. He enjoyed visiting other churches on fifth Sundays and listening to gospel music and helped preside during funerals and homecomings.

My father was a well-rounded person who knew the value of exercise and relaxation. He went fishing in the warm weather seasons and hunting in the cold. Listening to baseball on the radio or watching them on TV was enjoyable. When the Braves came to Atlanta, he attended many of their home games. So, of course, he was ecstatic when the Braves won the World Series in 1995 and wore his Atlanta Braves baseball cap with great pride. Boxing and wrestling were also some of his favorite sports.

He was incredibly proud of and loved his children, grandchildren, and above all, eternal love for his wife, my mother, "Lizabeth."

My Mother, Mrs. Elizabeth Nash Gorley and Children
Leila, Frances, and Robert, Jr.

My Mother, Mrs. Elizabeth Nash Gorley

My mother, Mrs. Elizabeth Nash Gorley, was a loving woman, and she was a hugger. She hugged and squeezed so hard; you would be glad when she let go.

They were married in 1936, and their marriage lasted 64 years. They had ten children, whom she loved unconditionally, and was so proud of us. She was always happy to either see or hear from us.

Mom worked in various domestic positions in her early life. She became a homemaker after having so many children. Mom was an excellent cook, a skill she learned from her mother. And boy she sure knew how to stretch and make do. She was raised primarily by her mother, Lizzie Binder Nash, after her father, Benjamin Nash, passed when she was very young.

Mom made quilts by hand and loved to sing, dance, and recite poetry, one of her favorite poems was "A Psalm of Life" by Henry Wadsworth Longfellow. She also enjoyed looking at fashion and Black magazines, including Ebony, Tan, Essence, and others.

In her youth, she attended the African Methodist Episcopal (AME) church, St. John AME, and attended alone for many years because we went to church with our Daddy, who attended Ebenezer Baptist Church. Although Mom always supported the Baptist church by sending food and attending special services, after constant urging by my Daddy, she eventually joined the Baptist church, but it was short-lived; she was AME at heart.

My siblings and I loved our mother and father and honored them by creating a legacy scholarship award, the Robert and Elizabeth Gorley Golden Handshake Achievement Award. We started the award for graduating high school seniors in our family with plans to further their education through college, trade, or vocational school. The award is our way to continue their legacy and commitment to family and education.

A MAN OF VALOR

And the Angel of the Lord appeared to him, and said to him, "The Lord is with you, you mighty man of valor!"

JUDGES 6:12

On July 19, 2022, my husband passed while we were in the process of publishing my book. Unfortunately, he didn't have an opportunity to read it. However, *Sunburst* would not be complete without sharing the story of my husband, Marcus Lowe, a man of valor.

"I don't care what people may say about me; I work for the Lord," Marcus always said.

He loves the Lord and firmly speaks these words. However, he seldom speaks these days, his beautiful smile remains. During his healthy days, Marcus served as an usher for many years at his church.

Marcus was born in Shelby, Mississippi, and was the youngest of four children. Marcus' mother, Pinkey Daniels Lowe, died of childbirth complications, so he was raised primarily by his father, Arvie, Sr., his stepmother, Willie, and several other relatives. He and his brother, Arvie, Jr., are the only surviving siblings, as Felton and Blondine are deceased.

Growing up, Marcus lived in three states, Mississippi, Arkansas, and Michigan. During the Korean War, Marcus was drafted into the U.S. Army on his birthday, something he always felt was unfair. When Marcus was discharged, he experienced the same scenario: no work for a young Black man.

Marcus worked for the top three automobile makers, Ford, General Motors, and Chrysler, only to be laid off when work was slow. He heard about better working opportunities in the aircraft industry in California. So, he and a friend headed West. He found work in San Diego, for a short time. But there it was again; he was laid off due to no government contracts. So, he decided to try his luck in Los Angeles, a much bigger city, and after pounding the pavement and many interviews, he was hired at Lockheed Aircraft Company in Burbank. His first assignment was washing aircraft parts before being placed on the assembly line, which was a very low-paying job. However, Marcus was not dismayed because he had his foot in the door, and by this time, he and I were married and had our son.

Marcus always wanted to improve himself; he attended West Coast Trade School and graduated with a certificate in custom upholstery. After receiving his certificate, Marcus applied for a position, "in cabin trimming," to work on aircraft interior, installing seats, curtains, and anything dealing with fabric. Unfortunately, Marcus did not get the job due to a lack of experience. However, he was determined to succeed, so Marcus persevered; with his union and the labor relations board, they challenged, "Mahogany Row" (Lockheed Management Department) pleaded his case, and Marcus was hired. He went from journeyman to senior lead man before retiring and received many quality assurance awards during his tenure at Lockheed.

Marcus is multi-talented. He is gifted at oil painting, doll making, floral arrangements, and ceramics. In addition, he was a high-scoring bowler and loved all sports, especially tennis and basketball.

I salute my husband, Marcus Lowe, a man of valor with an infectious smile and a sunny personality.

Marcus and Frances are the proud parents of Gregory and Melody, the grandparents of six children and the great-grandparents of two.

SECTION I

MIGHTY SHOULDERS WE STOOD ON—IN GEORGIA

CHAPTER 1
"Auntie"

Andrea Mae Gorley

My aunt, Miss Andrea Mae Gorley, "Auntie," was my father's sister and she lived next door to us with my grandparents until they died. Auntie was a schoolteacher. During my early years, she taught school out of town and came home occasionally. I can remember everyone being excited when she came home. My entire family was proud of her, and she was considered the "smart one." Auntie's brothers and sister contributed toward her education, which African American families did in those days. Auntie was married several times, but I only knew and remembered one of her husbands.

It was lots of fun growing up next door to my father's family. There were always a lot of different family members living at my grandparent's home. Aunt Lou and Big Auntie, two of my father's sisters went to New

York to work. They were part of the Great Migration. Each of them had two children and lived with Grandma Mag until they were old enough to be on their own. Once they became teenagers they went to live in New York with their parents. Auntie had two daughters, Annie and Dot, and they lived with my grandparents as well.

Below are the names of my other aunts:
1. Aunt Sarah—my mother's sister
2. Aunt Freddie Mae—my mother's sister
3. Aunt Roberta—my mother's half-sister
4. Aunt Eva—my mother brother's wife
5. Aunt Nola Mae—my mother's brother's wife
6. Aunt Edna—my mother's brother's wife (I never met this aunt)
7. "Big Auntie"—my father's sister
8. Aunt Lou—my father's sister
9. Aunt Willie—my father's sister

We had some cousins who lived in Atlanta who visited during their summer vacations and holidays. To us country kids, these cousins were "city-wise." They loved to make fun of us because we lived in the "country." We didn't have all the modern conveniences they enjoyed, such as indoor plumbing. Instead, we had an outhouse. An outhouse is a structure built outside with a seat with a hole over a deep pit—basically, an outside toilet with no plumbing. They were grossed out by having to use the outdoor toilet. My cousins talked about going to the zoo, swimming, roller skating, going to a park; Stone Mountain for picnics, and many of the things that children in our small town seldom had an opportunity to experience. Regardless, we loved them. We were happy when they visited and loved hearing about their city adventures.

Growing up as children, we were never alone. We always had someone to walk with us to school, church, or to the picture show (movies). In those days, there was safety in numbers.

At an early age, I can remember Auntie and other African American teachers in our small town going to Fort Valley State College in the summer to earn their teaching credentials and their bachelor's degrees. Another teacher, Ruth, who lived on our street, also went to summer school to work on her bachelor's degree. One summer, upon her return from Fort Valley State College, Ruth gathered all the neighborhood children and taught us the summer curriculum focused on exercise or what later became known as physical education.

Ruth showed us the tennis shoes that she had to wear when she exercised and ran. It was amazing to us because Ruth was quite overweight. We could not imagine Ruth running. It was hilarious. We laughed about her behind her back, as children will do. Even the grown-ups talked about Ruth's weight, many to her face. Some people said she had a problem with her glands. Very few people in our town were obese because of the hard labor and the amount of walking they did. At that time, most African Americans in our small town did not own a car.

As an adult, I respect and honor how much the African American teachers willingly shared with us children in our little community. We would listen attentively to what all adults said to us. We believed them.

When I talk with former schoolmates, they can still quote what different teachers would say to us. It is always a joy to have a conversation with my former classmates and friends, when I go to Eatonton. Our country needs more dedicated teachers like the ones we had many years ago. Teachers who are interested in each student. We need more teacher interaction with the communities. We knew we were loved, and our teachers wanted us to succeed in life. Our teachers taught us to avoid teenage pregnancy, getting into trouble with the law, and going to reform school. It was taught, and we believed that going to reform school (now known as juvenile detention centers) ruined your life forever.

Having to work in the sawmill or cut pulpwood, pick cotton, pick fruits and vegetables, or milk cows for a living seemed like a dead-end situation. Most women worked as domestics for extremely low wages. As opportunities were opening to African Americans, our teachers wanted us to be ready to seize the moment. Our teachers and school principal, Mr. McGlockton constantly told us, "Without a high school diploma you will not be able to get a job."

I loved math in school, perhaps because of my father's constant prompting. We were pushed to do our best in school. African American children were encouraged to leave Eatonton upon graduation. We were often told, "There is nothing here for you." Encouragement came at school, church, and in the African American community. Also, we were constantly told how to behave and conduct ourselves in public. Young girls were cautioned about the clothes they wore, especially shorts in public. If an adult observed us doing something inappropriate out in the community, they notified our parents, and we were disciplined.

Many African American teachers taught school without a degree in those days. I can remember when Auntie received her bachelor's degree from Fort Valley State College. Auntie was incredibly proud of her certificate, which she gladly showed us and displayed in her living room for everyone to see. I think it motivated many people who saw it. In addition, her degree enabled her to continue teaching once schools were integrated. Auntie was one of the first African Americans from Eatonton selected to teach after school integration.

Once some of the teachers came to Eatonton, they became a part of our community. Some of these teachers married people already living in Eatonton. After they were tenured, many purchase homes and joined local churches. Recently, I spoke to my sister, Jule, and asked her what happened to some of the teachers we had when we were students when the schools integrated. She said, "When their contracts weren't renewed, most of them left Eatonton in search of other employment."

Integration of the schools was a good thing. It was supposed to place everyone on an equal playing field. However, I wonder how integration affected the African American community because so many African American educators lost their jobs after integration.

Auntie loved children and after integration she was assigned to teach first grade. I was surprised by this because at one time, she had been a principal at a school in the rural county area. I asked her why she taught first grade and her answer was that it was the grade she wanted to teach. She had been given a choice and Auntie wanted to mold a child in their first year of school. She left a mark on so many students she taught, especially their handwriting. The printing of all these people resembles each other in every way—big, bold, and precise. I was never taught by Auntie, but she taught some of my siblings. Their handwriting is so much better than mine, and I find it difficult to distinguish one sibling's handwriting from another.

Auntie was awarded the "Teacher of the Year" of an integrated school.

This was quite an honor for an African American woman in the state of Georgia. She had worked extremely hard all her life and received many gifts and accolades, including the BGA also known as the "Big Golden Apple."

A few years ago, I had an opportunity to talk with one of Auntie's great-grandsons, and I happily shared my memories of her with him, I told him of her fine qualities and attributes I remembered, and I was sure she would have had high hopes for him and all her great-grandchildren. Auntie influenced many people to enter the great field of education, including some of her relatives, students, and others she met along the way. Today, we need more dedicated teachers like my Auntie.

I loved and admired Auntie and looked up to her. I have great respect for all teachers and educators. However, I never considered becoming a teacher. I think I can learn to teach, and I have the patience, but I do not have an outgoing personality to connect with children of all ages, day after day.

Children are very observant; they know when you know your job and are interested in their welfare. So, I would find teaching day after day to be very mundane. That is why I chose a career in nursing. I believe students deserve someone who is excited and fun to learn with them, someone like Auntie.

Auntie was a lover of all people. As a small child, I saw many African American senior citizens who could not read, or write come to her for help with their personal documents (old age papers) or to have her explain things to them.

Auntie was the only aunt in our family who owned a car and that could drive. She had a car before my father had one, she helped my father learn to drive. Auntie had a lot of courage. She was the only woman I knew who drove her car from Georgia to New York in the 1950s with just her children and young niece. Auntie never had a car accident, gotten a ticket or had a road encounter with other drivers.

On hot summer days, Auntie would pile as many children as she could in her car. If you're wondering how we all piled in the car with Auntie. The answer is, in those days, seat belts were not yet installed in cars.

We would go fishing and have picnics at a place known as Flat Rock. Usually, our lunch consisted of a bologna sandwich and Kool-Aid or a soda pop to drink. I can't remember having chips or cookies. All children should have the opportunity to experience carefree summer days. These were some of the best days of my childhood.

FLAT ROCK

As a young child, I have very fond memories of going to Flat Rock, with Auntie several times and with my daddy. Flat Rock is a rural area in Putnam County. It's a beautiful place with a creek and water flowing over the rocks.

Every year, our church, Ebenezer Baptist, hosted a summer vacation Bible school. The culmination ended with a picnic at Flat Rock. It was a much-anticipated event that we children looked forward to, because we traveled by a chartered bus. Riding on the bus was a joyful experience. It was a time to be with your friends. We sang as we rode along and could not wait to play in the water.

I loved being in nature. We would play in the shallow water and jump from rock to rock. Unfortunately, none of us had swimsuits and few people could swim. Those who could swim were boys; they learned to swim in the creek or the river, as we did not have a swimming pool.

Georgia is a very green state, with tall pine trees, green grass, flowers, and different plants growing wild. We would see many kinds of birds and beautiful butterflies flying around and bees buzzing from flower to flower. Occasionally we would see lizards and frogs. Once with our father, we saw a big black and white striped snake. He was alive, but he just laid very still as we walked past him.

In my eyes, the eyes of a child, Flat Rock was a true paradise. Flat Rock was beautiful, simply beautiful. Unfortunately, I have not visited Flat Rock since childhood, therefore, I do not think I would recognize it today. I hope someday to revisit Flat Rock.

Before 1953, Flat Rock's source of water was from a creek known as Crooked Creek. At that time, in the Flat Rock area was only a church and some houses. There was a grassy area where people could fish and picnic. Lake Sinclair was created in 1953 when the Oconee River was dammed to create a hydroelectric generating station, it was huge project. Participants included the Oconee Area Planning and Development Commission, the U.S. Forest Service, the Georgia Game and Fish Commission, Georgia Power Company, and several independent businesses. Today, Lake Sinclair, with its small beach, is a popular recreational area. There are facilities for picnics, grilling, boating, and waterskiing. In addition, Lake Sinclair is the site of several fishing tournaments and lovely homes along the waterfront with boats tied up in their front yard.

THE WIT OF AUNTIE

Auntie was very quick-witted. One summer day, she had taken many of us to Flat Rock for a day of fun. We went out on the creek fishing and playing in the water. Some of the older children were fishing, without a fishing license. Suddenly, the game warden, a white man appeared. We were surprised and frightened at the same time. We had not heard or seen him coming until he was right up on us. We all knew the job of the game warden. He just stood there staring at Auntie and all of us. We all watched Auntie closely for a clue about how we were to respond. He didn't say anything. She looked him right in the eye and said,

"We are just trying to catch some fish for our dinner."

"Are all these your children?" The game warden asked.

"No, not all of them, but I am keeping some of them for the summer so their parents can work."

He stood there thinking for a minute or two. I imagined he thought: *This colored woman with all these children could not pay a citation, so what would be the use of giving her one.*

He scratched his head and said,

"Okay, I hope you all catch some fish for your dinner." And he walked away.

I remember looking at Auntie and thinking how clever she was to avoid a citation that day. I wanted to be smart just like her. I hope to always have an answer, and never just stand there looking ridiculous when in a confrontational situation.

Several teachers who taught in Eatonton were from out of town and they often boarded with local families because there were no rentals available in Eatonton. Having to work in the sawmill or cut pulpwood on menial wages, many African Americans rented and never owned property. Several lived in what we called the "little red houses." These houses had only two rooms, with no plumbing nor electricity, in the early days. One man owned these houses and he rented them to African Americans workers.

Auntie was a very sociable person. Her home was a gathering place. We would watch her visitors' cars from our yard. We knew we better behave because our Auntie was friends with all the teachers and sometimes, they would come over to visit. Also, she was extremely popular among people in town. She loved to cook and entertain guests from our community. Often, after eating one of her delicious meals her guests would talk about the world affairs or play cards games.

Auntie played music, but I never knew her or her guest to dance. She smoked cigarettes, and occasionally she had a "government" drink. We called it a government drink when alcohol is sold in liquor stores rather than bootlegged or homemade. Some southerners referred to legal alcohol as "sealed liquor."

There never was any loud noise, disorderly conduct, or anything out of the ordinary happening at Auntie's house. Neighbors never had to call the police to Auntie's home.

As I mentioned before, Auntie's home was a gathering place. She had a television before most of us in our neighborhood, and her living room floor was always full of kids, especially when our favorite shows came on. Two of our favorite shows were *The Ed Sullivan Show* and *I Love Lucy*.

The Ed Sullivan Show gave African Americans the chance to see celebrity African Americans perform on television. We were proud to see them, and we could never get enough of watching our people express our culture. Some of the top names we loved to watch were Fats Domino, Chuck Berry, Nat King Cole, Dinah Washington, Ella Fitzgerald, Duke Ellington, and Harry Belafonte. Our favorite young singers were Little Richard and Ray Charles, both Georgians. Little Richard was born in Macon, Georgia, and Ray Charles was born in Albany, Georgia. Even with Elvis Presley crashing on the scene with his hip-shaking moves, we preferred our hometown heroes. We looked forward to seeing these shows and made sure we always completed our chores and homework before going over to Auntie's house to watch TV.

Another favorite show was *Amos 'n' Andy*, and I cannot forget to mention *The Little Rascals*, also known as *Our Gang*, was an American comedy series of short films telling the adventures of a group of poor neighborhood children and their adventures. This comedy series was produced from 1922 to 1944. The show broke racial barriers by showing white and Black children interacting as equals, which was amazing for that time. Today, some Americans think this show is degrading. However, these actors were our heroes, and we could hardly wait for them to come on TV or see them at the picture show. We loved Buckwheat, Spanky, Alfalfa, Porky, and the whole gang.

Next, is one of the favorite stories our family members loved to tell. It was told often, especially at gatherings and always with lots of humor. The cousins loved to share it because our cousin, Dot, was the one who got everyone in trouble.

THE CHRISTMAS COOKIES

One year just before Christmas, the adult family members went to Macon, Georgia, to do some Christmas shopping. While they were gone, the older children used the ingredients in the cupboard; flour, sugar, butter, eggs, and all else needed to bake cookies. Later that night, after the adults returned, our cousin, Dot, asked Mom Mag for some more cookies. Mom Mag told Dot there were no cookies in the house. Dot kept insisting she had eaten some cookies earlier in the day. She finally told Mom Mag that Annie, Bobbie, and the rest, had baked cookies while the adults were gone to Macon. By then, it was late, and everyone was in bed. Mom Mag discovered all the Christmas ingredients she was to use for baking had been used up. Mom Mag was very angry; she was smoking hot. In the middle of the night, she came over to our house and told our parents about baking cookies, which meant making a fire in the stove while no adults were home. It was dangerous. My older brother, Bobbie, and my sister, Jule, got a big whipping by our daddy, right then and there. I didn't get a whipping because everyone knew I had a "bad heart," and plus I did not bake the cookies. My "bad heart" finally caught up with me later in life—I now have a pacemaker.

THE BAD HEART STORY

I was born a tiny and weak baby. The old country doctor told my parents I had a bad heart, and I would not live long. So, for years I was treated with "kid gloves." Every time I was about to be punished for doing something wrong, I would cry, "You know I have a bad heart." Sometimes it worked and sometimes it didn't. Many times, I would run over to my grandmother's house next door. Mom Mag, as we called her, usually gave me candy when no one else was around, with the warning, "Don't tell anyone!" My beloved Mom Mag died just before Christmas when I was in the second grade.

Auntie was a faithful church member, and for many years she was the church secretary. When I was a child, she was in charge of the Easter program that included reciting a speech in front of the church congregation, participating in a play, singing, and an Easter egg hunt the following Monday. We would start rehearsing at Auntie's home, but as Easter was nearer, we went to the church to practice so we could get accustomed to standing up in front of a live audience.

One Easter, Lewis, a young boy in our neighborhood, struggled with his speech, he had a learning disability, and he wanted to participate in our Easter program. Auntie had worked with him practicing repeatedly. Unfortunately, there were no special education programs for disabled children in our schools. Most were sent to public school and passed on year after year until they dropped out. These children never had the chance to learn a skill or a trade, which would have made their lives so much better. Many of these children's, especially African Americans, lives were lost.

After much coaching, Auntie said, "Lewis, when they call your name, go up to the front, place one hand in front of you, and the other hand behind your back, bow and say, "Happy Easter, Happy Easter." She was never one to embarrass anyone or look down on anyone.

Another example of her kindness was when, one Sunday, a man who lived down the street came stumbling by as we were sitting on Auntie's front porch. He had been drinking too much. So, he stood on the street just cursing and staring at us.

In a very firm voice, Auntie said, "Joe, go home and lay down; today is Sunday." Joe dropped his head and just walked home down the street without saying another word.

EASTER AT EBENEZER BAPTIST CHURCH

The members of Ebenezer Baptist Church started preparing for Easter the Saturday before Easter. First, the boys would go to the barbershop for haircuts, polish their shoes, and some would get new shoes. Next, some would get new suits, shirts, and ties. Otherwise, they have their suits cleaned and shirts laundered. Finally, all clothing would be laid out or hung up to be ready for Easter Sunday.

The girls would start doing their hair. Those who could afford it went to the beauty parlor and those who could not afford to go to the beauty parlor got their hair done by their mother, sisters, or friends who would do hair in the home. Either way, all the little girls wanted "baby doll" curls or "Shirley Temple" curls.

Most girls got new dresses and shoes for Easter, and some got little hats, purses, and gloves. Our parents sacrificed a lot so their children could have a new outfit at Easter, along with an Easter basket and eggs.

Easter was an important day at Ebenezer Baptist Church. We all gathered in great anticipation on Easter Sunday. Almost everyone dressed up in their new Easter outfits and some children carried Easter baskets.

All the parents and extended family members came to see the children recite their speeches, sing, and participate in the Easter evening program. It was the church's highlight of the year.

Lewis arrived all dressed up and wearing a bow tie, fresh haircut, and his little round face shining. We were all waiting anxiously for his name to be called. When his name was called, many of us were scared for him and held our breath. Lewis went up front, bowed, and slowly said, "Happy—Easter,—Happy—Easter." The audience gave Lewis a great big applause. All of us children were so proud of him. I am a "Easter" person.

Ebenezer Baptist Church is one of the oldest and largest African American churches in Eatonton, Georgia. It has a long, fascinating history.

Slavery ended in 1865, and in 1866, a small number of African Americans started holding their worship services on Sunday in the White Baptist Church. Reverend Isaac Brannon and Reverend Sill Carter were the first two pastors. Reverend H.F. Oliver, who was white, served as the moderator.

Over time, the African Americans wanted to be more independent and worship God under their own *vine and fig tree*. So, a few Christian-minded and judicious citizens arranged for the African American congregation to start their own church. An organized meeting was held in the basement of the White Baptist church, located where Eatonton Grammar School now stands.

As a result of the meeting, Ebenezer Baptist Church was born.

Reverend W.M. Green was called to be the pastor.

The church continued to grow under different leaderships. The first church was built on the land where the home of Mr. Albert Adams now stands. This church included a school that had one teacher. A second church was built on a tract of land secured from Mr. Green Williams. It was a large comfortable church that served the congregation for several years.

The growth of the church was phenomenal. Under Reverend H. Taylor's administration, the church thrived. On the second Sunday in May 1880, thirty-six people were baptized. The membership continued to grow; a decision was made to build yet another church. The current church was built for $4,000. Rev. F. M. Simmons was the pastor at that time. In 1991, the church saw the need to add a Fellowship Hall. Rev. Matthew Dennis was the pastor at the time. The construction was carefully done to preserve the historic structure. In 2021, Ebenezer Baptist Church celebrated its 155th anniversary and is debt-free.

During the early years, gospel singing was extremely popular and still is today, Auntie would drive the children who were in the church choir to various churches to sing.

Another activity we had as children were to learn all the books of the Bible. This competition was mainly for the males in the church. The Sunday School Superintendent was Mrs. Leila McAden, a retired schoolteacher. One year my oldest brother, Bobbie, was in this competition. He told us how Mrs. McAden made him stay at her house late one night until he could recite all the books of the Bible with 100% accuracy. This was the year Ebenezer Baptist Church's Sunday School traveled to Ebenezer Baptist Church in Atlanta, Georgia for the convention. It is the home church of Dr. Martin Luther King, Jr. Unfortunately, I can't remember how my brother scored.

Auntie loved Ebenezer Baptist Church, so much so, she became a self-proclaimed evangelist. She would go out into the country and drive people to our church, hoping to grow our church's membership. In addition, she provided clothing for some of these people and in turn they would give her food and chickens.

My grandparents, Auntie's parents, were sharecroppers, and because she had grown up on a farm, she never forgot her farming skills. One Fall morning, my parents killed a hog, When Auntie came home from teaching school, she took off her school clothes, and came over to help my mother clean chitterlings, which are hog intestines. She knew how to make hog head cheese and cracklings but she never seemed to mind getting her hands dirty.

As long as I can remember, Auntie planted a vegetable garden every year. I know because we went to her yard to pull weeds for a nickel. Besides having various animals, including chickens, ducks, rabbits, and dogs, she had a pecan and a quince tree (A quince is a fruit similar in appearance to a pear but rarely eaten raw; best when eaten cooked). Auntie was a lover of flowers, and she had a wide variety of many types of flowers and plants. Now, when I go to Eatonton, I find it hard to believe that many people don't have vegetable gardens, small animals, and chickens. Auntie was very thrifty, and our family often joked about how many meals she could get out of a chicken by including the neck and the feet.

On my father's side of the family, Auntie was my favorite aunt. I have some of her traits. I love flowers and plants. I once had a small vegetable garden in my backyard while living in Los Angeles. I always enjoyed talking with Auntie and this continued throughout her life. After I was grown up, I would call her on the telephone and talk for hours. I was glad when the telephone companies began "unlimited talk" for a flat fee.

Whenever I visited home, I would spend a couple of nights in her home, and we would talk about many things. She would tell me all that had gone on in Eatonton: births, weddings, deaths, who had a new house, who had gone to college and so on. Auntie always knew the latest news. I suppose this could be called gossiping.

In 1973, Auntie came to California. It was wonderful having her visit me. She was full of wisdom and knowledge. As I sat writing this book, I still have so many questions. I wish I could pick up the telephone and talk to her, it would be wonderful.

While Auntie was visiting me in California, we went shopping. She loved stylish clothes and wanted to see what California had to offer. Auntie bought me a bracelet, which I still have, and she bought my daughter, Melody, underwear with little red hearts. She was in the first grade at St. Michael's Catholic School and, she wore the new underwear, Auntie bought for her to have a "Show and Tell" at school. That evening I received a telephone call from Sister Rosemary asking me to teach my daughter that she must not "show and tell" at school. The joys of motherhood!

Our beloved Auntie entered eternal rest October 19, 1981. Her legacy: two daughters, five granddaughters, six great-grand-children, three sisters and three brothers, and many relatives and friends.

"Well done my good and faithful servant," Andrea Mae Gorley.

CHAPTER 2
The Great Migration

The Great Migration was the relocation of more than six million African Americans from the rural South to the cities of the North, Midwest and West from about 1916 to 1970. Driven from their homes by unsatisfactory economic opportunities and harsh segregationist laws, many Black Americans headed north, where they took advantage of the need for industrial workers that arose during the First World War. During the Great Migration, African Americans began to build a new place for themselves in public life, actively confronting racial prejudice as well as economic, political, and social challenges to create a Black urban culture that would exert enormous influence in the decades to come (Source: History.com).

MY FAMILY MEMBERS THAT MIGRATED

My father, Mr. Robert Gorley, Sr.'s siblings:

    Uncle EC—moved to Chicago, Illinois

    Uncle Buster—moved to New York, New York

    Aunt Lou—moved to New York, New York

    Big Auntie—moved to New York, New York

    Auntie Willie—moved to Atlanta, Georgia

Only my father and Auntie remained in Eatonton

My mother, Mrs. Elizabeth Nash Gorley's siblings:

    Uncle Harvey—moved to Minneapolis, Minnesota

Uncle Bud—remained in Eatonton, Georgia
Uncle Edward—moved to Macon, Georgia
Aunt Freddie—moved to Minneapolis, Minnesota
Aunt Sarah—moved to Boston, Massachusetts
Only my mother, Aunt Roberta and my Uncle Bud remained in Eatonton, Georgia.

In addition to my uncles and aunts migrating to other states, many cousins and friends also migrated to other states.

As you can see, several of my family members were a part of The Great Migration. Unfortunately, I didn't have the opportunity to know much about many of my uncles and aunts. What I have heard is strictly hearsay (gossip), so I choose not to repeat any of it. However, I am mentioning them out of love and respect.

As for my mother's side of the family, I saw my Aunt Freddie Mae and Uncle Harvey only once during my lifetime. They both came to my grandmother's Lizzie's funeral, when I was in the third grade. On my father's side of the family, I saw Uncle EC and Aunt Lou only once as well, at Auntie's funeral in October 1981. I was an adult with two children. I don't know how they earned a living, whether they owned property or could drive a car. As someone who also migrated, I often wonder, were their lives improved by leaving Georgia? This question remains unanswered to this day. However, I know my life improved greatly by migrating.

CHAPTER 3
A Toast to a Great Man

Let us raise our glasses to Professor Wright N. McGlockton, a long-time principal of the African American school system of Putnam County, also known as the Eatonton Colored School System.

Mr. McGlockton was an average-looking African American whom we seldom saw smile. He was serious and always wore a coat and a tie. He also wore white socks, which you could see because his pants were too short. On several occasions, when the superintendent would visit our school, he would display a deep sense of appreciation and humility.

Mr. McGlockton had a practice of calling the students by their last names. I cannot ever remember him calling me by my first name. My brother Robert was "Gorley," my sister Leila was "Gorley," and I was "Gorley." My younger siblings said they were all called "Gorley."

He was born in Colbert, Georgia, graduated from Morehouse College in Atlanta, and was known as "A Morehouse Man." Mr. McGlockton did his graduate studies at Atlanta University and had served as a school administrator at three other public schools before coming to Eatonton, Georgia. He was a special gift, and we were lucky to have him in Eatonton,

During Mr. McGlockton's administration, Eatonton's public school system greatly improved. There were no gymnasiums during the early years. Classes were held in many African American churches, old rundown buildings with little heat, poor lighting, and no indoor toilets. In addition, and as I previously mentioned, many of the teachers did not have college degrees. Much of this changed under his leadership.

My first encounter with Mr. McGlockton was when I entered first grade. I knew who he was because he had visited our home regarding my older brother and sister. In the early days, principals like Mr. McGlockton went to the students' homes to talk with their parents. These visits did not mean students were in trouble. Instead, he aimed to meet with the parents to get to know their families.

My parents always wanted our family recognized in a positive light. Our small, modest home had to be clean and in order, and we always had to be on our best behavior. African Americans in our community had great respect for teachers and principals, and our parents' valued education.

I was a shy and clinging child. The first few days of school I went to my older sister's classroom before going to my own. I suppose her teacher eventually called Mr. McGlockton to remove me from my sister's classroom. He came right in and physically carried me out. I remember kicking and screaming as he took me back to my first-grade teacher, Mrs. Gladys Sanders' classroom.

Our school did not have a kindergarten class. I was not too fond of Mrs. Sanders because she wore glasses, and her eyes were misaligned; the medical term is strabismus (cross-eyed). Mrs. Sanders looked over her glasses at me, and as a six-year-old child, I was terrified.

She spent lots of time trying to win me over. So much that I soon became known as the "teacher's pet." I was constantly teased a lot by my classmates and other students. Some of the older students tried to frighten me and would often taunt me; now that would be called bullying. They would say, "You won't be the teacher's pet when you get to Mrs. Williams' class. Mrs. Williams is very mean, and she will beat your butt, and she can hit hard."

In Mrs. Hankins's second grade class, I learned to behave and avoid punishment. I can't remember getting in too much trouble in her class.

Meanwhile, I had that "appointment" with Mrs. Williams in the third grade. It was true what they said, she could hit hard. I observed this when she disciplined the boys. However, she never hit the girls as hard. I only received one spanking from Mrs. Williams; otherwise, we got along just fine. I think she liked me, and I learned to like her.

Each Christmas, Mrs. Williams gave a prize to the student who had good conduct, did their schoolwork, had perfect attendance, and practiced good hygiene. However, she gave two prizes in my third-grade class. I was fortunate to win one. I was surprised she had selected me because I had received a spanking before Christmas and was forced to sit in the corner in disgrace. The prize was a box with three handkerchiefs inside: white with tiny, embossed flowers that were blue, pink, and yellow. Those handkerchiefs encouraged me to try harder, behave, and do my best in class.

The other student, a girl, received a box of handkerchiefs with a different pattern. A mean girl, the class bully, teased me because the other girl's handkerchief had a little gold color fringe around the border. I didn't care because I felt so lucky to have received this prize, even after getting in trouble. I moved on to the fourth grade, thinking Mrs. Williams was not as mean as reported.

One day we were outside for recess when Mr. McGlockton drove onto the school campus in his old beat-up station wagon. It was loaded with several crates of big red delicious apples. Then, we all watched as he single-handedly unloaded the crates of apples and put them into his office. I learned to be thankful for this simple treat.

Later that day we were called to line up at the front door of his office to receive a big red delicious apple, our treat.

For whatever reason, Mr. McGlockton always impressed me. He not only unloaded those crates of apples by himself, but he also made sure we were able to have some. He was one of the most generous, compassionate, and dedicated educators, I ever knew other than Auntie.

We went to the home economics department a few days later and were treated to warm applesauce. Several times during the school year, they provided special treats such as candied apples, hot chocolate, and donuts. I can still remember the taste of the nutmeg in the doughnuts. I have a suspicion the delicious treats were government surplus food. However, no one ever mentioned it, and we happily ate them.

Miss Cook was in charge of the home economics department for many years. She taught us many things; however, I remember her mainly for teaching morals and her strict teaching about cleanliness. Miss Cook and the older students prepared the desserts. It was a good learning experience for the older students and a treat for us.

Occasionally, Mr. McGlockton would address the entire student body at what was known as "the chapel." He pressed upon us how hard he worked to graduate from high school. He told us how he had to get up early to work at a sawmill before walking to school. Afterwards, he walked back to the sawmill and worked until dark. Working in a mill is hard, dirty and grueling work. He described not having decent clothes and shoes and how he persevered. The message here was, "You can make it if you try." If a person works hard, they will reap the benefits in the years to come in the form of a check, a house, a car, food, and the desires of your heart.

Mr. McGlockton and his wife, Rosa, did not have any children. In many ways, we were their children. Mr. McGlockton humbled himself to get whatever he could for our school from the Board of Education. He was not what some folks in town would call an "Uncle Tom." An Uncle Tom is an offensive word used for a Black man who was considered excessively obedient to white people. Mr. McGlockton was a real father figure to us.

I read somewhere that our school received used books that were in good condition from the neighboring white school. We used to take the used books home and make book covers for them out of brown paper bags. We cherished these books and were grateful for each of them.

We read the *Weekly Reader* to keep up on current events around the world. Unfortunately, I find today that many young people and adults do not have a clue of how our government works and who are our government officials. Some have no concept of geography or history; however, they know the latest news about entertainers, athletes, movies, and music. A young coworker told me, "I don't clog my brain up with unnecessary things; when I need to know something, I just Google it." It's proven to be true on several daytime talk shows.

When I traveled abroad, our tour guide told us many Americans travel to other countries without reading, researching, or knowing anything about where they are traveling. Another criticism of Americans was that many of us don't speak other languages, but we expect other countries to speak English.

I am thankful for those used books that taught us so much about our world. In high school, I was a very avid reader. I enjoyed reading about many things, particularly about people and food. My favorite classes were history and geography.

While growing up in Eatonton, the only people I saw were either White or Black. However, I was very curious to learn about the cultures of Native Americans, Japanese, Africans, Eskimos, Chinese, or those I thought to be more exotic than us in Eatonton. An example, the word "siesta" was often used in Western movies. I thought, *Do people actually take a nap after eating lunch every day in Mexico?"*

I love all types of food. The food I read about had unfamiliar names: pizza, avocados, filet mignon, tiramisu, escargots, asparagus, fettuccine, lasagna, tacos, burritos, guacamole, to name a few. Then there was Scotch and other liquors on the rocks. I used to think, *what is on the rocks?*

Reading influenced my love for different types of food. In my opinion, a great place to sample unique and delicious food is on cruise ships. Chefs from all over the world work on them. The food price is included with your fare, which is a bonus because you get to try all of it. You can always send it back without discussing the cost if you don't like it. When I go, I always order food that I have never eaten before because some buffets are plentiful, but not so appetizing. I have sampled many foods that I never knew existed throughout my lifetime. I hope that I continue this practice.

As a teenager, I was very intrigued with martinis. It was the name that attracted me. I just knew it had to be a fabulous drink. I often saw martinis served in movies and TV, and men usually consumed it. When men would come home from their office jobs, their wives would make them a martini to help them settle down and relax. Men would also order them at bars. When I was of age to drink, I ordered one too. I was extremely disappointed and never drank another one again. It was not what I expected, and it was not my kind of drink. However, my curiosity was satisfied due to my engagement with those books passed on to our school.

I was removed from the classroom a second time by Mr. McGlockton when I was a junior in high school. I was in home economics class when suddenly Mr. McGlockton entered the room with a piece of paper in his hand. He read out the names, and mine happened to be on the list. He told us to get our things and come with him. It made all of us nervous. Every fall, students in home economics were afforded what we thought was a day of freedom and adventure at the State Fair in Atlanta. I had gone to the fair the year before and enjoyed the festivities. We were worried that Mr. McGlockton was going to take away this privilege.

We had no choice but to follow him, and to our surprise, he escorted us to the typing classroom. The class was not full and needed more students. So, he chose students who he thought would benefit from typing class the most. I don't know why or how he selected us. Maybe he used a crystal ball, and he could see our futures. There were about four boys in the class and the rest of us were girls. I am not sure if the boys were unhappy about being placed in a typing class. We were assigned to take typing as well as Gregg shorthand. I passed shorthand, but I was never mastered it. I do not remember anything about it today, not one thing. As a sixteen-year-old, I did not see a good reason for taking business classes. I hadn't seen anyone who looked like me typing in any of the businesses around town. So maybe the teachers thought we should move up North to get a business job. At that time, the thought of leaving home frightened me. Yet a few years later, I moved to a city much larger and further away than Eatonton, Los Angeles. There, I was able to get a job typing. Plus, after graduating from Sawyers Business school in Los Angeles, I worked in the clerical field for over ten years before returning to college to pursue nursing.

When I started using a computer at work, it was easy because I knew the keyboard by heart. However, I was scared at first. My son, Gregory, encouraged me and taught me how to use a computer. Mind you, Gregory was teaching me over the telephone all while he was in the Army. I have since taken a few computer classes, and many people are surprised that I can use Microsoft Word and Excel. Many seniors are afraid to try to use computers. Some people have asked me: *how did a Black girl from rural Georgia learn to type?* Some folks think people in Georgia only knew how to pick cotton. When I have compared my school experience with other people from The South, I'm amazed at how advanced Georgia is ahead of other Southern states. An example, my friend from South Carolina told me they had to pay for coal to heat their classroom and they had to pay for used books.

One of my classmates Hattie excelled in typing and shorthand. She loved it. Years later, when we reconnected, she told me our typing instructor was her role model, and she wanted to be just like Miss Ellis.

I will admit our typing instructor was very inspiring. How she dressed, talked, and her whole personality represented what every modern Black girl wanted to become.

Miss Ellis was a city girl, a lady with class, from Atlanta, Georgia. She always wore very high-heeled shoes and straight skirts. She strutted when she walked, and you could hear her heels clicking down the hall.

After graduation, Hattie moved to Washington, D.C., where she worked at the Pentagon as a secretary to a top military officer. The class paid off for both of us.

BUTLER-BAKER SCHOOL

As a result of Brown v. Board of Education, government officials in Georgia built a "state-of-the-art" public school for the African American students in Eatonton. In 1956, the new school, Butler-Baker School, was named after two prominent African American citizens of Eatonton: Mr. W. T. Butler and Mr. William Baker. Mr. Baker and his family were the first Black dairy farmers in Putnam County, and Mr. W. T. Butler was involved in religious and educational affairs.

The cost of the school was $500,000. The new school had a science lab and a business curriculum that included typing and shorthand. The old school had an agriculture and home economics curriculum, and these programs were extended. The home economics program, instructed mainly by Miss B.B. Cook, introduced many students to washing machines, clothes dryers, electric irons, electric stoves, and electric sewing machines. In addition, the male students had an opportunity to learn vocational skills. It also had a library, and Mrs. Rosa McGlockton was its first librarian.

Butler-Baker had two outstanding music programs, and before long, it soon got its first marching band. I can proudly say I was a band member, and I played the clarinet. It was the only marching band in Eatonton. Even the white public school didn't have a band at that time. I don't remember how many members were in the band, but we had seven high-stepping majorettes. On February 20, 2020, these seven ladies were honored for breaking glass ceilings. Their names at the time were: Georgia Benjamin, Leila Gorley, Virginia Gorley, Lucy Hogan, Mary Howell, Doris Reid, and Mozelle Reid under the leadership of our band director, Mr. Kennedy. A few years later Mr. Bostic, became our band leader. It was so much fun to show off our marching skills downtown Eatonton.

Butler-Baker students were privileged to study under the guidance of Mrs. Mayfield, a college-trained music teacher. At the time, many people who played in churches or locally throughout the community played by ear. Mrs. Mayfield could sight-read music and play by notes. She taught us music theory and music history, and we learned about great composers, such as Bach, Beethoven, Chopin, and many others. She had a wide range of skills and talents.

We also learned about voice. In our small town, several students had great voices but no training. Mrs. Mayfield encouraged them all. We became optimistic that someone from Eatonton would make it big. However, I don't know anyone who made it professionally in the music field aside from Mr. Bostic, who played the trumpet professionally. Often, we could hear Mrs. Mayfield playing and practicing on the piano at school, as she did not have a piano where she was living. Occasionally, she and Mr. Bostic would play together.

A JOB WELL DONE

The growth and high standards set by Mr. W. N McGlockton help Eatonton schools to be held in the educational field on both the state and national level as an example of progress, due to his personal leadership and integrity.

- Mr. McGlockton was held in high esteem by both whites and Black people in the educational field.
- Mr. McGlockton genuinely believed education was the key to success. Under his leadership the percentage of 12th grade graduates increased.
- Mr. McGlockton had three main objectives:
    - The Student
    - The Teacher
    - The Parents
    - He encouraged parents to give extra time and labor for the benefit of the school and community.

- "Most of all, we are trying at Butler-Baker to teach citizenship. We want students to be better boys or girls because of having gone to school here. We want Eatonton to be a better town because of our work." —Eatonton Messenger, August 21, 1956.

- Mr. McGlockton was a giant of a man, a Morehouse Man. He was a man for the time yet a man before his time. He was futuristic.
- Mr. McGlockton was able to retire and enjoy his farm for a few years. He passed away April 2, 1970.

"A key is both a tool and a symbol, a tool in its everyday use,
a symbol in opening the door to hidden mysteries
and knowledge in the fields of learning."

—A. C. Dickey, School Superintendent.
Stated at the Formal Dedication of Butler-Baker School
Source: Eatonton Messenger, February 24, 1957

Butler-Baker School

CHAPTER 4
"Miss Sweetie"

In 1950, Putnam County's population was 4,982. My hometown is seventy-five miles south of Atlanta. Most of the people were either cotton farmers or dairy farmers.

Many of the African American people could barely read or write. African American women often found employment in the white community homes as domestics. Other women did laundry at home to make ends meet, my grandmother Mag was one of these women.

African American men found work cutting pulp wood, working at the sawmill, milking cows or some types of cleaning jobs. There were a few men that found work in the factories, as janitors. In addition, there were the independent workers such as barbers, beauticians, brick layers, funeral homeowners, café owners, painters, handy man services and small store owners.

Also, there were the religious occupations—preachers and ministers. Many of the independent workers catered only to the African American community. I am using the term African American however, at this time, the terms "colored" or "Negro" were used to describe African Americans or Black people.

The first school I attended had no flushing toilets, all grades went to one little wooden shack, with wood and coal burning stoves for heat. As we grew older it was a student's responsibility to keep the fire burning, usual it was one the boys that took care of this. On certain days, all the students went out on the school grounds to pick up the trash. This was customary, no one grumbled or complained—we just did it. We learned responsibility at an early age.

There was no changing of classes. There were no science labs, microscopes, typewriters, lunchrooms; none of the finer things of education. There were no playgrounds with swings, slides, or seesaws. We played in the dirt and went home dirty. Our recess activities consisted of the boys' shooting marbles and the girls' jumping ropes, playing hopscotch, hide and seek, Little Sally Walker and the horse and buggy.

So much was different in those days. We had a cloakroom where we all placed our coats, boots, hats, and umbrellas. At the end of the school day, it was one of student's responsibility to pass out the items to the correct student. We were assigned this activity in advance so we would know when it was our turn. This simple task taught us how to work and be responsible. Although simple, some of the students that graduated from this little country school have done extremely well in life.

Years later, I relived part of my childhood when I saw students at a catholic school in California doing the same things I did as a student back in Georgia. I served as a eucharist minister at my local parish church mass and the school student body mass once a month.

When mass was over, older students folded the chairs and placed them on the cart. The older children were assigned a "little buddy." It was their responsibility to keep the younger students quiet during mass, take them to the restroom, if necessary, and explain what to do during mass, such as when to stand up and when to sit down. The students learned to clean up after mass. I did not observe one student at my church who did not participate or complain. So, you can see some practices of training children are still being handed down even in different states and many years later.

"Train up a child for the way he should go and when he is old,
he will not depart from it."
—Proverbs 22:6 KJV

Early in my first year of school, a white lady came to our little school to give children our "school shots." These shots had such strange-sounding names—diphtheria, measles, and smallpox. So many students, especially the boys, made fun of the word pox, and I don't know why.

The nurse came to our school to give us shots, because we were at school, and it was easier for her to come to us. Most of our parents did not have a car to drive us to a clinic. My mother and many other African American women in my hometown never learned to drive.

As a first grader, I was very fascinated by the nurse. Back then I thought her name was "Miss Sweetie" because I repeated what I thought I heard. I remember her wearing a little white cap. I wanted to wear a little white cap just like hers and one day I made a little cap out of paper and wore it at home. In my little head, I was "Miss Sweetie."

She always looked fresh, clean, and crisp. I often reflect on why I was fascinated by the nurse's uniform. Was it the white uniform, white stocking, white shoes, a little white hat, and the Navy-blue cape with red lining or something else?

Although, I grew up thinking her name was Miss Sweetie, I learned in 2020 from my older sister that her name was Mrs. Bessie Sweda. I am not sure how many other people thought the same as I. It was Georgia after all, and Southern people constantly "mispronounced" words.

As with most children, I was afraid of shots. If we had known when she was coming, many of us would have played sick and stayed home.

However, Miss Sweetie was always kind and gentle with all the students when she gave us our shots. I did not cry, I wanted to I wanted to be a "big girl." The boys would joke and say she had a big needle, and she was going to break the needle off in our arms. Of course, this never happened.

Recently, I read in the Eatonton Messenger Newspaper an account of her retirement, and many people referred to her as "Miss Sweddie." So, you can see she was Miss Sweetie to some and Miss Sweddie to others. She was a great nurse. Miss Sweetie set a bar so high few could jump over it. She accomplished a lot in her life, far too much to write about here. She generously gave of herself as the first public health nurse of Eatonton.

Miss Sweetie worked alone for many years and traveled many rural miles to bring healthcare to many people. In those days, very few people had health insurance. She was a very special gift to the people of Eatonton.

The article dated March 27, 1969, read that Mrs. Sweda began her public nurse career in 1949. It was very inspiring to read the articles and see her photo. I read how she had trained twenty midwives to help women bring life into this world. It took a lot of love, skill, and patience. Growing up, I knew many African American women who were midwives, so I assumed many of the midwives she trained were African American. As children, we believed the midwives had babies in those little black bags they carried. As children we believed when we saw "Mom Liza" going to someone's house, she would leave a baby. "Mom Liza "delivered me, her name is written on my birth certificate. Looking at that old black and white photo of Miss Sweetie bought back many fond childhood memories.

Since I knew Miss Sweetie as a child, my memories of her were limited. I remember hearing people praise and trust her to help and take care of them. Recently, I have read several accounts of her work. Based on this, Miss Sweetie was a "universal person," which meant she respected all white, Black, or other people. No matter if they were rich or poor, she saw a need and she responded.

While trying to get information regarding Miss Sweetie, someone told me this story:

This woman's young son was outside cutting grass. He came into the house crying to her in pain. He had big blisters on his shoulder. She thought fire ants had bitten him. She described the blisters as "big as a teacup." She did not have money to take the child to a private doctor. Her first thought was to consult with Miss Sweetie. She took her son to the public health clinic. Miss Sweetie told her what to do when she got home. The primary instructions were to prevent the spread of the infection. The mother was to keep the area and child clean. The child's shoulder wounds healed with no complications.

The mother saved a doctor's fee, which would have been difficult for her to pay. Just imagine what could have happened to the child if there had not been for Miss Sweetie. There was no Obama Care back then.

These school visits with Miss Sweetie went on for a few years. As the economy progressed, in 1952 Putnam County built a public health clinic.

Each year around June and July all students had to go to the clinic to receive their immunizations for school. Unfortunately, many of the students missed having Mrs. Sweda come to our school to see us one on one. Going to a new building was different from lining up with your classmates, crying, talking, and having Mrs. Sweda's full attention.

I can remember vividly going to the clinic with my mother or my older siblings. On my first visit to the clinic, I felt scared and insecure. Even, as a young child, I could feel the difference of going to a clinic. I imagine that all the children and their parents from our community had to adjust to going to the clinic.

The public health clinic offered other advantages for the low-income people of Putnam County. Pregnant women could go to the clinic to receive prenatal care. Young women learned about nutrition, vitamin supplements, and birth control. Babies could go to the well-baby clinic for care. Many seniors with diabetes received patient teaching regarding insulin injection, foot care, and proper dieting. People with hypertension learned how to manage their high blood pressure medicines and diet. Many African Americans have hypertension, and it was important for them to learn about salt intake and its effects.

With knowledge and education, the health of the citizens of Eatonton improved.

Today, this clinic has increased its services to include HIV testing and high-risk infant follow-up. The clinic also has a hypertension clinic, CPR, TB assessment, STD assessment, a resource library, physical assessments, car seat safety classes, WIC (A Special Supplemental Nutrition Program for Women, Infants, and Children), COVID-19 testing, and many other programs for the people of Putnam Country.

SECTION 2

STRONG SHOULDERS
I STOOD ON—IN CALIFORNIA

CHAPTER 5
Bessie and Charles

CHAMPAGNE TASTE

I met Bessie and Charles when I was eighteen years old. I had just arrived from Georgia, the Peach State. Bessie and Charles were old enough to be my grandparents, and I respected them as such. Bessie had one daughter, Mary, who was the same age as my mother. Mary's two older children were close to my age. Charles had one son, and he was older than I. However, I do not remember his age. His son, Chip, never married and had no known children.

Bessie and Charles had been married to other people. Charles's first wife was deceased, and I never knew what happened to Mary's father, Bessie's first husband.

I interacted more with Bessie than with Charles. Our relationship was more of that as a grandmother and grandchild. Mary, her husband, and youngest son lived in the rear apartment. Mary styled hair for friends and family members in her apartment to earn extra money because she did not work outside the home. Bessie encouraged me to let Mary press and curl my hair. I made sure to shampoo my hair before because Mary only pressed and curled. I mostly wore my hair in a ponytail with a rubber band holding it together during that time. Bessie would often complain that I should take care of my "messy" hair.

Both mother and daughter took me under their wings. Bessie and Mary advised me on fashion. They would tell me what colors matched my skin color, where to find clothes on sale, and how to use the layaway. Back then, I was small, which made it easy for me to find clothes in my size.

Bessie lived in an old two-story, five-bedroom house. She rented out four of these bedrooms to earn money. Together, Bessie and Charles built an apartment building on the rear of their property. Old Los Angeles have huge lots, so people would often add income properties in the back of their homes. Bessie and Charles were both unemployed senior citizens when I met them. After moving to California, Bessie was a domestic worker, and Charles worked on the railroad as a porter.

As the old saying goes, one could say that Bessie had a "champagne taste and a beer pocketbook." She used the money from their income property to buy expensive and beautiful things from home furnishings to clothes, shoes, furs, and hats. I don't know for sure, but I can assume they had lots of debt because Bessie was often short on money.

Bessie had spent lots of money on her old house. She updated the house's original white wooden exterior to medium pink stucco with white trim. She remodeled the bathroom by adding blue tile, added cabinets to her kitchen and put windows in her breakfast room. Everything Bessie did was first class, and it was beautiful in its day. Bessie's home was a showplace. As an African American teenager coming from rural Georgia, I had never seen African Americans living on such a grand scale. Bessie's furniture was all antique. She had very exquisite lamps with very fancy lampshades, custom-made drapes in her living room and dining room, a huge formal dining room, and wall-to-wall carpet throughout her home.

Before the Watts Riots, there was a street named Santa Barbara in Los Angeles, California, but now it is called Martin Luther King Blvd. There used to be some expensive furniture stores there. Many of these stores were looted and burned down during the riots. One of these stores was called Barker Brothers, a chain store with locations in expensive places like Beverly Hills, California. Only the "high class" shopped there.

Barker Brothers closed in 1992, leaving an interesting history. I remember this store because Bessie had furnishings from there in her home.

In the 1960s, many people in Los Angeles had what was known as a "picture window," a large glass window in the living room. At night people would open their drapes for people passing by to look into their homes to show their luxurious furniture, with elaborate lamps as the focal point. Today, this is unheard of in our society. If you drive by and see homes in Los Angeles, you will notice many have iron bars on the windows because people are more afraid of thieves than showing off their picturesque living rooms.

Bessie and many of her friends were originally from the Midwest. Though they migrated across the country, they remained friends. Their children were friends with each other, and so were the grandchildren. However, I observed none of the grandchildren married within the circle. Bessie and her friends followed the same regiment as long as I knew them. They were Baptists and attended church every Sunday morning. After church, they would go to each other's homes for dinner, and later, they would sit around talking and watching TV.

When it was Bessie's turn to host Sunday dinner, she would spend lots of time cleaning and getting everything pristine. She would enlist all of us to help her clean with the promise of a free meal. I first learned of a rump roast from Bessie, it was her favorite dish to cook for Sunday's dinner, and it went well with gravy, mashed potatoes, and string beans.

Early every morning, Bessie and her friends would call and check on one another, speaking briefly. In many ways, they did this to make sure their friends had lived through the night. They were extremely close, like family instead of friends. These friends were always there for one another. None of these ladies could drive, they would ride the bus for however long checking to see if someone was sick. If someone died, they made sure to take care of the bereaved. Likewise, they were there for each other in happy times such as births, birthday parties, baby showers, weddings, and more.

Just like they were there for their friends, they were there for me. After Charles and Bessie attended my wedding and I moved to another side of town, we made sure to stay in contact. They were both alive when my children were born, and Bessie hosted my baby shower when I had my daughter. Over the years, as they got older, Charles became disabled. Since Bessie could no longer care for him, she placed him in a nursing home, where he later died. Sometime in the late sixties, Bessie went to live with her sister in another city, and I lost contact with her. That was the last time I would get to see her. I always wondered what had happened to her circle of friends. I was grateful for their friendship.

Bessie and Charles influenced my life in so many ways. I picked up some of her good habits and some of her bad. For example, we brought an old house, which we could afford. We were starting out, and real estate was expensive in Los Angeles and still is. But, like Bessie, I was not satisfied and did upgrades like painting the exterior. My father was a house painter and always kept our house in Georgia well painted.

How I wished he was there!

I wanted my house to look cared for as well for as my parent's home. I was somewhat ashamed of my house because the paint was peeling off, and it was noticeable. Also, the fences around the property were wooden and needed replacing. It was an expensive project, but I did it anyway. I was working, so I convinced my husband to paint the house and replace the fences.

It was also a mistake. I should have waited. Other things needed to be repaired or replaced. My wants mounted. Like Bessie, I put my family in debt.

Today, I can see some of the "Bessie influence" in my home. For instance, there was a round glass table in Bessie's breakfast room, and I have one in my kitchen, too. Once, I had some fancy drapes in my living room and dining room too, but I learned how expensive they are to upkeep. As they aged, I replaced them with less expensive ones. I appreciate fine and antique furniture, but I have never bought any. However, I did learn the value of good furniture. I always wanted to have a breakfast room with large windows. I wanted to have a pleasant view as I sat, drank coffee, and read my daily devotions. Today, I have a sunroom where I read and meditate, but it has no view.

Bessie used the phrase "tickey" to describe order and cleanliness. As I age, I find myself being "tickey." I want my house neat, clean, and in order. Over the years, I saved too many things that maybe I should have gotten rid of. Now wiser, I want all the clutter gone. So, I have become "tickey," as well.

On the other hand, I never found a close-knit group of friends to go to church with, have Sunday dinner together, or talk to each day, if only to check on our well-being. Though I have friends, we do not share many of the same interests, do not go to the same church, and our busy schedules and family obligations keep us unavailable. Therefore, that part of my life can never be like Bessie's.

With Bessie and Charles, I always felt welcomed and a part of their family. They were there to help me become an adult. I will never forget them and their family members for the kindness and generosity they showed me, a teenager migrating from Georgia. Bessie and Charles will always be my foster parents.

CHAPTER 6
Sister Sam

"Lord Make Me An Instrument of Your Peace."

I met Sister Samuel, a nun affectionally known as "Sister Sam," during my first nursing job. The Sisters of Penance and Christian Charity founded St. Francis Medical Center in 1945. She was the heart and soul of St. Francis Medical Center. Sister Sam had already advanced in age when I met her. Her habit was to work many days before sleeping, as people often had to put her to bed.

She could barely walk and just shuffled along, but Sister Sam was a powerful force to be reckoned with. In addition, she had a powerful personality, always smiling as she walked throughout the hospital.

It was the hospital's practice to give all the employees gifts at Christmas. Therefore, the lower-paid employees received a more valuable gift than the higher-paid employees. For example, I received a flashlight one Christmas, and some lower-paid employees received a blanket. The hospital stressed that the higher-paid employees should always be kind to the lower-paid employees. Sister Sam said, "we had been blessed to be in our positions."

Each day Sister Sam would pack the leftover food to give the lower-paid employees to take home to their families. She oversaw this task herself. Staff that worked the night shift could eat a meal at no cost. As a result, food was never wasted at St. Francis Medical Center. Hospitals cannot practice this today because of spoilage, the risk of food poisoning, and lawsuits.

On one occasion, the RN staff had a safety training class: The training was given by the laundry supervisor, an African American. He spoke to us about safety, things to watch for, such as needles and dentures that may have been accidentally placed in the linen hamper. The nursing instructor had nothing but high praise for this individual. She complimented him on how clean the linen, towels, washcloths, and other things were laundered. In those days, the sheets had to be folded uniquely. The seams of the sheets had to lined up perfectly with the center of the bed.

Everyone at St. Francis was expected to treat each other with dignity and respect. Doctors did not yell at nor threaten the nurses there, as I have witnessed at other hospitals. St. Francis had extremely strict standards. The people I worked with did their jobs very well. I don't ever remember anyone telling me some gossip or complaining about their job.

Recently, out of curiosity, I googled St. Francis Medical Center, and I was very shocked to read some of the reviews people had posted. It's hard to believe they are factual. Over the years, there has been a decrease in women entering religious life. Therefore, lay people are in charge of many Catholic hospitals, and many have closed their doors for several reasons. When I worked at St. Francis, the Sisters emphasized human dignity, compassion, service, and respect.

However, their Mission and Value statement reflects that same dedication of years past:

Our Mission:
To deliver quality care to patients
and better healthcare to the community.

Compassion:
We deliver patient-centered healthcare with compassion;
dignity, and we respect every patient and their family

Quality:
We are always providing exceptional care and performance.

Community:
We are honored to be trusted partners who serve,
give back and grow with our community

It is the New St. Francis Medical Center Leadership

PHYSICIAN-LED

St. Francis Medical Center is a uniquely physician-led organization that allows doctors and clinicians to direct healthcare at every level. Working at St. Francis was a spiritual experience for me. The priest said a prayer over the public address system every morning. The prayer started with "Good Morning, God." Before breakfast, a bell would ring, a signal that the priest was bringing Holy Communion to the patients. We were taught to cease doing whatever we were doing until the priest and the nun passed. We often saw the nuns praying their rosaries as they walked the hospital corridors. A young nun played the organ during the day, and we often heard her playing soft, soothing, beautiful music.

Sister Sam loved to make a special cake she called Harvey Wallbanger. This cake required vodka and liqueur Galliano. She always found people willing to supply her with these special ingredients, as she shouldn't have been seen going into liquid stores. Once in a while, Sister Sam, would proudly announce she had stayed up all night baking Harvey Wallbanger cakes. Then, she joyfully served her cake to all the staff. NOTE: Once the cake is baked, and as with any food that contains liqueur, the alcohol can no longer intoxicate a person—the alcohol becomes inactive. It is just a flavor.

My most memorable event with Sister Sam occurred when she called me into her office one morning. I was surprised by how fast news traveled at St. Francis Medical Center. It seems some big ear was listening when I was insulted by a college nursing professor.

In the Bible, Luke 12:3 reads,

"What you say in the dark will be brought to the light."

Therefore, one should always be careful. What you say, you never know who is listening.

I was still a new nurse when this incident occurred, as I was preparing to give a patient his morning dose of insulin. A professor rudely took the insulin bottle and syringe from my hands. She said, "My student will give this insulin." However, she didn't ask if it was okay with me or not. Sister Sam told me that Julie, a young, registered nurse, who was being groomed as an assistant head nurse, reported it to her. Julie was beautiful, intelligent, and energetic. She had a sweet disposition and was well-liked by the staff and respected by the doctors. I was not aware that Julie had witnessed this incident. Sister Sam was known for integrity and she expected honesty from those working around her. Knowing Julie's popularity, I was astonished that she had stood up for me, a rookie Black nurse!

I said to Sister Sam, "Yes, it happened."

Sister Sam said, "Dear, all you have to do is say the word, and she will never come here again."

It was powerful to realize that I had so much power in my first nursing job, as a young African American nurse was sometimes overwhelming.

Sister Sam reminded me that I was a St. Francis Medical Center employee, and the nursing professor was not. Also, I was a registered nurse who had passed the California State Board examination, which was a big deal. I had never been elevated to such a prominent position in my entire life.

Before giving Sister Sam my answer, I thought long and hard about this situation. Of course, I could get the professor, in trouble with the college, but what would be my reason? I thought, *would it be because she insulted me, or would I try to get back at her to show my power?*

Recently, I was thinking about this incident; at the time, I was a new nurse. I was sympathetic with the students because, having been a student myself, I didn't want the students to be prevented from coming to St. Francis Medical Center because of something the professor had done. I remember Sister Sam looked at me for a very long time before speaking, and she understood my compassion.

The truth is that Sister Sam knew I was too scared to do it. She blessed me with my decision and said, "I hope you have a lengthy career in nursing. May God bless you, child." Life has many twists and turns. I saw the same nursing professor working at another hospital some years later. She was not working as an instructor but as a staff nurse. I recognized her, but she did not indicate that she recognized me. I have tried to practice what I learned at St. Francis Medical Center throughout my entire nursing career; be kind and show compassion.

Because I worked at St. Francis Medical Center, I know my life is so much richer. My interactions with Sister Sam, the people I met there, and all the experiences taught me to be generous, to care about my less fortunate brothers and sisters, and most of all, to have self-respect.

I can now understand why I often find it difficult to understand some people I have encountered in life. So many people have not had the humane experiences I experienced at St. Francis Medical Center. It's up to us who are blessed to lead the way.

THE LESSON:
Be generous, be respectful, be compassionate,
value yourself and value your self-worth.

MY PRAYER:
I pray Sister Sam reached paradise where she is smiling and joyfully
baking her beloved Harvey Wallbanger cakes!

CHAPTER 7
Injustice

It is 2022, and it is difficult for me to see the racial injustice and social unrest that the United States is experiencing. Looking back to the 50s and 60s, I think I lived in a better time. During segregation, Black people had limitations, but I don't think we had the fear that African Americans are experiencing today. All older adults, both Black and White, were respected. People did not curse in front of the elderly. People allowed the elderly to go first. Unfortunately, today, many people do not practice common courtesy; I find this unbelievable and amazing. Recently, I heard someone constantly say, "who raised you?"

As an African American mother of a son and grandmother to two grandsons, all Black males in my family and all in America, it was very frightening to me to witness the police officer murdering George Floyd on national TV. The murder took place in plain daylight and with someone videoing. The police officer appeared confident that he would get away with murdering George Floyd because of the racial climate in the United States. Back in the day, this activity was reserved for the dark of the night, with robes and face coverings. But, while growing up in Georgia, I never felt the fear many African Americans express today. I believe one of the reasons I was less fearful was because most Black and White people knew each other. As I previously mentioned, my father was a well-known house painter, and my auntie was a public school teacher, so they both connected with many people. As with my father and auntie, people were known for their reputation, character, and morals. I also believe that when people are hardworking, good church-going citizens, it provides an umbrella of protection. For example, people would say something similar: "you're Henry's son; I know Henry." It was remarks like this I heard as a child growing up in Eatonton.

During the 1960s, my generation believed if we went to school and worked, we could also achieve our piece of the "American Pie." We had positive role models. John F. Kennedy's administration established many programs to enable the low-income citizens, like the Manpower Job Act. I graduated from business school under this program. In the 1960s, voices cried out for justice and equal opportunities for all. Our country was on the right path in the 1960s and 1970s. It was a very progressive time for America. During the 1960s, the latter years of the Great Migration, I followed my brother to California. Many of the people I met were from out of state like myself. The people I associated with were looking for a better future. I met these people either at work or school. We went to school at night, and some worked two jobs.

I observed and learned from my co-workers and classmates. For example, one co-worker faithfully saved part of her paycheck, and in a short time, she went from riding a bus to buying a car. A few years later, she bought a starter house. I know a lot of stories like hers.

I had a supervisor, Mr. Carl, who had grown up in the Great Depression, he constantly told us how to save money and bring our lunch. He would say, "When you receive a raise, save it, don't spend it. Launder your clothes, don't go to the cleaners unless necessary."

Mr. Carl had so many tips for us. His wife cut his hair, and he did not go to the barbershop. When he retired, he paid cash for a huge motor home. On his last day at work, he joyfully told us, "I am ready to live and see America!"

Many people from Putnam County, both Black and white, have done exceptionally well. Putnam County has produced outstanding inventors, writers, doctors, and lawyers; some are world-famous. Through education and hard work, African Americans from back home now enjoyed many privileges such as owning property, owning businesses, annuities, 401K's, savings accounts, health, and life insurance, paid vacations, travel, and being able to educate their children.

Strangely, it was the famous Watts Riot that influenced me to go back to school. I was married with two children and worked in an office, mostly with women of all ethnic groups. Only White men held high positions. There were only few chances for upward job mobility, especially for African Americans. One day at lunch, a co-worker told us about a college being built primarily to educate and train African Americans living in South Central Los Angeles, California. It was big news.

The Watts Riot occurred on August 16, 1965. On August 11, 1965, an African American motorist on parole for shoplifting was pulled over for reckless driving by a California Highway Patrol motorcycle officer. According to community members, an argument broke out and escalated to a physical confrontation. The driver, Marquette Frye's brother, who was a passenger in the car, walked home, which was nearby, and returned with his mother, Rena Price. The situation continued to escalate. There was physical contact between law enforcement, Price, and her two sons.

Community members reported that law enforcement officers had roughed up Frye and kicked a pregnant woman. These rumors spread throughout Los Angeles. Finally, angry citizens began throwing objects at law enforcement officers and arrested Rena Price and her two sons.

The community was in an uproar. The police department and local Black leaders held a community meeting on Thursday, August 12, to discuss an action plan and urge calm in the Watts community. Unfortunately, the meeting failed to find a solution. Meanwhile, the rioting grew.

The government officials called the National Guard to come help quell the violence. Unfortunately, some used this as an opportunity to commit crimes, loot stores, and burn businesses to the ground. Due to this riot, people in Los Angeles lost thriving and beautiful properties, including African Americans who owned thriving companies in South Central Los Angeles; some of which have not been rebuilt. Many White business owners fled the area, which became known as "White Flight."

The Watts Riot changed South Central Los Angeles. So much was lost, never to be the same. Thirty-four people died, 1,032 were injured, and 3,438 were arrested—the property damage estimated at around forty million dollars.

The United States has gone through a significant period of turmoil in the last few years. Some are:

1. Global pandemic, COVID-19
2. Presidential Impeachment of Donald Trump
3. Internal attack of democracy of the United States
4. Social unrest
5. Economic crisis
6. Oil crisis.
7. Homeless crisis

November 2020, America elected the oldest president ever—President Joseph Biden. He had several personal losses during his lifetime, yet he persevered. Mrs. Sweda never gave up on her dream to help people. The lesson here is to defer your dream if you must, but never give up.

CHAPTER 8

My Journey to
Becoming a Registered Nurse

I moved to California to to get a better education. However, my path to nursing was not smooth. I was young and not prepared, educationally, for nursing school. During that time in California, many nursing schools were in hospitals, and registered nurses could train and receive their diplomas from these hospitals. It gave them hands-on experience, making them at the top of the nursing hierarchy.

The Associate of Arts nursing program was still in its infancy stages when I started college. Some people thought nurses needed more hands-on training and did not trust a program for two-year registered nurses. I had taken business classes in high school but had not taken the required science classes, such as chemistry, physics, and Spanish. In Putnam County, French was the only language offered.

I was allowed to take my entrance exam at a local hospital. Though I passed the written test, I was rejected because I did not have the required courses. I had to fall back on my business skills, and as a result, I passed the Civil Service examination. I was blessed to have always been able to get jobs without going on many interviews.

Rumors were floating around at work that one of the clerks had gone to college at night and received an AA degree. When she took her certificate to the personnel office, she immediately received a promotion. So naturally, my co-workers and I were excited; several of us went and enrolled in evening classes. I began taking general education classes. I had not really decided what it was I had hope to accomplish. I had considered starting a daycare in my home as I had a rental property and Southwest College had such a program.

Later on, a pre-nursing student convinced me to work toward getting into the nursing program. She sold me on the idea by saying, "the salary was great, and nurses will always be needed."

I was afraid to try to enroll because of my earlier failure. This classmate and some others were working in a hospital, and she encouraged me with these words, "Just hang with us, and you will get through."

I had done well in the general education classes, but I feared the sciences. Again, lucky for me, I met people who wanted to form a study group. At Southwest College, some African American teachers met with our group and tutored us. These teachers were often from the South and understood what we had gone through in school. They too had similar experiences and made sure give to us the support we needed.

The semester that I was taking anatomy, I was placed in a group with two other students. One was a surgical technician, she was our leader, and the other student was a nurse's aides. We were assigned to dissect a cat. We were to tie off parts of the cats and label them. Whenever the professor walked by to check on us, he often said he was impressed by our work.

Our instructor was a very interesting person, he had worked for NASA, on the project that developed food for the astronauts and he brought in some samples for us to see. It was very interesting information.

On the final day when we were to present our cat, it was missing! Someone had stolen our cat. However, we got an "A" because the professor had already observed our masterful work.

I took all the pre-nursing classes at night while working full time during the day. Luckily, I didn't have to take any foreign language courses for this program. However, I took chemistry, microbiology, anatomy, mathematics, physiology, public speaking, English, history, and political science. When I completed all the required classes, I applied and was accepted into the nursing program.

The nursing program was highly stressful for me as I had two small children. My son had a life-threatening illness during my first year of nursing school. Thankfully, he fully recovered. As a wife and mother, I had lots of responsibilities. My father's first cousin, Lucile, would sometimes come on the weekend to help do my children's laundry, which allowed them to have clean clothes for school days.

Our nursing program was primarily adults, many with various amounts of medical experience. Unfortunately, some of these people created problems in the classroom. Because they worked in the hospital, they tried to dominate the class and instruct the instructors on what to do and how to do it. As a result, these people had to be reminded of who was teaching the class.

The two years of nursing school were interesting. I learned so much about human behavior. I met some of the most challenging people while taking nursing classes. On one occasion, some students formed a group and reported the teachers to the chairperson for showing favoritism. Students questioned and compared their grades. Southwest helped prepare me for challenges I would meet in the hospital setting with both the patients and staff. In my junior year, I was voted class president. That year my class sponsored campus bake sales to raise money for our capping ceremony. In my senior year, I made the Dean's List.

As I said, my classmates were working in medical-related jobs such as surgical-technicians, certified nursing assistants, psychiatric technicians, and licensed vocational nurses. It was a diverse group of students. Some of the students were over than 40 years old. Some of the women had as many as five children. There were a lot of different personalities. I am sure this challenged the professors. Overall, we had a dedicated group of students; very few dropped out. When a student was failing, other students and teachers supported them.

When it was time to take the California State Board, we formed study groups and studied for long hours and over several days. Our hard work produced few failures.

After graduation, I was so excited; I passed the California State Board on my first try. I always tested well, but it was my dedication that led to my success. I found employment right away and was selected for a one-year nurse internship program at Saint Francis Medical Center.

At one point in my career, I considered public health nursing. However, I didn't like to drive and still don't like to drive especially in the Los Angeles traffic. So, I chose to remain in the acute hospital setting for my entire career.

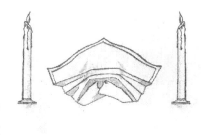

The Senior Nursing Class
of
Los Angeles Southwest College
Request Your Presence
At Their
Capping Ceremony
To Be Held At
Imperial Heights Community Church of The Brethren
1909 West Imperial Highway
Los Angeles, California
September 14, 1973
7:30 p.m.

Los Angeles Southwest College
Capping Ceremony Announcement

Candlelight Ceremony Procession

Frances Lowe receiving her
Nursing Cap 1973

Frances Lowe, Graduation photo 1974

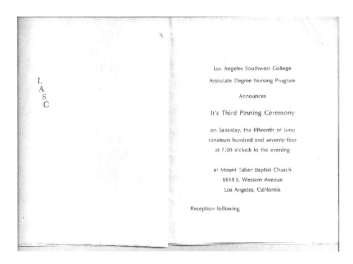

Los Angeles Southwest College Pinning Ceremony Announcement

Nursing has been rewarding, and my favorite task was wound care. I enjoyed taking care of difficult wounds and seeing the progress of healing. Also, it was rewarding to see previous patients in public, recognize me, and tell me they were doing well.

One morning we did not have any milk in the house. So around 5 a.m., I went to the 24-hour supermarket near our home. I noticed this man waving to me as I was driving, but I did not recognize him or his car, so I kept driving.

My mind was on the fact that I needed to get the milk for my children, find a parking space near the door, and outrun him. I parked, and as I got out, he called me by my name and said,

"Don't you remember me? I was your patient."

"What bed were you in?"

"Number 340"

"Oh yes."

"I just wanted to tell you I am still wearing my white socks as you told me to."

CHAPTER 9
Greatness

Throughout my nursing career, I worked with hundreds of nurses. Listed are many great nurses I know. I can't name them all, but I know many great nurses that do not have RN behind their names, yet they are outstanding people.

GLORIA HIGHTOWER, RN

Mrs. Hightower was a retired U.S. Army veteran and a registered nurse. My first encounter with Mrs. Hightower was early in my nursing career when she was my patient. At the time, I was working the midnight shift at the Veteran Administration Medical Center. I do not remember why she was a patient, but she was alert, very talkative, ambulatory, and did not require much nursing care.

Our conversation went something like this, "Little girl, I think you are a good nurse, but you can become a great nurse. There are nurses who can close one eye and hit a vein or can pass out several medications in record time, and many can do other things very well, but none of these things make them a great nurse."

She went on to say, "To be a great nurse, one must demonstrate to their patients that they really care about them. Your full attention should be focused on the patient, not glancing at your watch while talking to them. A great nurse takes time to really listen to their patients. Most of the patients here are men. A great nurse should know what interests most men. Most men want to know about sports. They want to know about their favorite team, they want to know who won the game. Just because you are a woman does not mean you should not know these things. As you are driving to work, listening to your car radio, know what is going on in the world."

My husband liked sports and kept up with them; therefore, it was easy for me to keep up with basketball, football, and boxing. On my off days, I often sat and watched TV with him. Occasionally, we went to sporting events. The Los Angeles Lakers were my favorite team, I watched them every chance I had. I didn't understand football, but I knew the most popular players. Boxing was also easy to understand; everyone knows what a TKO means. Also, I kept up with baseball; I knew which team was winning and the most popular players.

Most of the patients spent a great deal of time watching TV. Many of them would ask me if I watched certain shows and my opinions. They all seem to like comedy shows. A few were interested in politics. Religion was another hot topic we were told not to discuss with the patients. If a patient had a spiritual need, we were to get a referral for a chaplain to visit the patient; we were not to be a "Do It Yourself chaplain," which means preaching to the patient.

I only had contact with Mrs. Hightower that one night, yet she left a lasting impression that has stayed with me all these years. Throughout my career, I tried to smile and greet each patient by their name, even when the name was difficult to pronounce. If I could not pronounce the patient's name, I always asked the patient for the correct pronunciation of their name.

I remember one patient with a most unusual name that was difficult to pronounce, by at least 90% of the nursing staff. Being careful not to insult the patient, we finally decided to call him, "Mr. K." I asked him how he learned to spell his name and he answered, "I learned to spell my name right away, because it was my name."

I was careful with jokes because some people take jokes the wrong way. We had to be cautious of racial, sexual, and homophobia-type jokes, which may be funny to one person, but offensive to another person.

NEW YEAR'S EVE AND THE NURSING SUPERVISOR

One New Year's Eve, I was assigned to work the evening shift. Many nurses had called in on this particular day to start their holiday parties. Our staff consisted of two RNs and one CNA, (Certified Nursing Assistant) and the nursing supervisors could not get enough staff to cover the wards adequately. One specific ward had thirty acute medical-surgical patients. Many of the patients were diabetic; they needed glucose checks and insulin. Nearly everyone had an IV and IV medications in addition to their regular pain medications. Some of the patients had dressings that required changing every shift. We had several patients who needed to be fed or assistance with their meals. Some patients required assistance to the bathroom; other demands, such as a request for freshwater and help with the TV. Some were trivial things but had to be taken care of. We were swamped. If one of the patients had fallen or there was a code blue (cardiac or respiratory arrest), it would have been an absolute nightmare.

In desperation, I called the nursing office for help. The house supervisor, Miss Lewis, a retired Air Force nurse, came down from the penthouse to help us. She was wearing her clean, crisp white uniform, white shoes, and stockings. In one hour, Miss Lewis took the vital signs on fifteen patients and changed the dressing on a leg amputation. She helped set up some of the patients for dinner. In just one hour, the ward had calmed down. Before she left, she promised to go upstairs, check the staffing sheet to see if she could find someone to come help us.

Right after Miss Lewis left, the CNA told me that was going to the liquor store down the street because she wanted to buy some liquor for New Year's. I was outraged. I knew that trip would take about 25–30 minutes depending on traffic. This hospital was in a heavy traffic area. I could look out of the window and see nothing but bumper to bumper traffic on the freeway.

I told her, "No, you cannot go, how will it look to the supervisor if she found out, she will have my head. Stop on your way home. The liquor stores are open until 2 a.m." We got off work at 12 midnight, plenty of time to stop at the liquor store.

In essence, I was the charge nurse; responsible for the entire ward, in addition, I was the RN assigned to the total care of fifteen patients. The other RN was responsible for the total care of fifteen patients. The CNA was assigned to help the both of us. In normal circumstances there would be two RNs and two CNAs, and possibly a LVN (Licensed Vocational Nurse) to pass the medicines, depending on the acuity of the patient load. All the employees are entitled to a 30-minute lunch break and two 10-minute rest breaks. In this situation, it was my judgement that she should not leave the premises of the hospital in case of an emergency. She could go to the break room or to the cafeteria for lunch and breaks. In case of an emergency, she could hear the announcement.

As promised, Miss Lewis called in a LVN to come in early to help us. What a difference one person can make.

ROBIN, THE BEST NURSE

One day, a highly respected doctor approached me and said, "If ever I am a patient in this hospital, I want Robin to be my nurse. I know she will give me excellent care. I have watched her for several years, and I see how she takes care of the patients." Robin was a CNA.

I observed Robin; she was always upbeat, neat, and clean, and never complained about her assignment. Robin was well-liked by the staff and patients alike. The nurses could rely on Robin to report any patient problems to them. All the nurses wanted Robin on their team. Her assigned patients were always clean, their rooms were orderly, and they had all the necessary items such as water, straws, fresh clothes, toothbrushes, toothpaste, mouthwash, and at their bedside. I recently was a patient in a local hospital; the CNA never brought me a patient care kit that included a toothbrush, toothpaste, mouthwash, and other hygiene products. I had to request water and a washcloth. These are required items for all patients and should be at the bedside when admitted. The CNA's responsibility is to prepare the patient's room before admission.

One day as we were working, Robin confided in me that she had to flee from her native country. Robin became a refugee because she feared being killed. She told me, "I may never be able to go home again to see my family. I have a daughter back home living with my parents. My husband was killed; he was young. So, you see, I have had a sad life, but I am happy to be living in the United States. I can send money home; one day, I hope to get my daughter here." Robin and her daughter could have been "Dreamers." I hope one day, Robin and her daughter will be united.

ALICE, THE LEADER

A nurse who was on a particular ward had to go on jury duty, and I was assigned in her place for one week. I didn't know any of the nursing staff on this ward. However, I had seen some of them around the hospital. I was to work the night shift, 12 a.m. to 8 a.m. The first night the LVN and the two CNAs kept talking about Alice and how they missed her.

One CNA told me, "Tomorrow night you will see how different it will be, because Alice will be here, you will see how we work." I didn't know Alice. As for as their job performance, I had no complaints, they did their work.

I was anxious to meet this much talked about lady. The next night the staff consisted of three CNAs and two RNs. The LVN from the night before was off. When Alice arrived, the two RNs and two CNAs were already in the report room. Alice was a middle-aged African American woman. All the staff started greeting Alice loudly and very warmly. I watched Alice closely to see what made her so special. Alice simply smiled and acknowledged everyone and quietly sat down.

When the report was over, the three CNAs got up immediately and started preparing the ward's cart with towels, sheets, gowns, pads, etc. Next, they began making rounds on the patients. They checked all the patients, cleaned them as necessary, turned the bedridden patients, and put out fresh water. This made our job as an RN so much easier; we could concentrate on our medicines, orders, and charts because we knew an effective team was taking care of the patients and would call us if they found something out of the ordinary. By no means did it relieve us of our duties to make our rounds.

When they had finished with the entire ward, they took their break, and each took turns, answering the call lights. The RNs did not have to tell them what to do; they had their own routine. One male CNA worked very well with the two female CNAs, and he, too, was very cooperative and respectful. I enjoyed working with them. It was not a stiff or awkward situation; I can remember all of us laughing about something on several occasions.

Alice was a quiet lady. She had a sweet disposition, very respectful when she spoke, and I concluded it was the motherly quality about her that made her so special. Alice smiled a lot, spoke softly, and worked right along with the other CNAs; although Alice was the senior employee, yet she did not try to 'boss" the less senior employees. Sometime during the night, the RN, I was working with confided in me that even though Alice was going through a difficult time in her personal life, she came to work every day, did outstanding work, and maintained a positive and pleasant attitude. However, I was very saddened to hear later that Alice had become seriously ill and died in a short time. I was happy to have met Alice.

BEN

In the early 1970s I met Ben, an African American man, who worked as a CNA on the midnight shift. He was a veteran and had proudly served in the U.S. Army during a time of war. He was known as a fun-loving person off the job, but he had a reputation for being very dedicated to his job and dependable. Ben seldom called in sick or took an emergency leave. He treated everyone with respect. Ben would use his break time to visit his co-workers if he heard one had been sick, a family member was sick or died, or any misfortunate event. These were affectionately known as Ben's rounds.

Ben is memorable because he shared with me that while serving in the Army during one December, he had to sleep in a fox hole for many days. He said enemy fire pinned him down, and one of those days included Christmas. Ben promised himself that if he returned to America alive, he would never work on Christmas, and would do something to make other people happy.

Ben had a party on January 1st every year. In December, special people were invited to "Ben's party." Not everyone Ben worked with was invited to his parties; however, my first year on the job, I was invited. I was told to schedule myself to work the day of the party. I really didn't know what to expect—a party in a hospital? I organized my work so I could go down to Ben's floor for a few minutes.

He had the food catered and it was delicious. The menu consisted of fried chicken, sandwiches, potato salad, cake, chips, cookies, and soft drinks. Ben made his party so unique by placing new money, fresh from the bank, in a dish, and each guest was invited to take money from the dish. He wished everyone happiness and prosperity in the coming year.

Ben told me when we first met that he never worked from Thanksgiving Day through New Year's Eve. A new supervisor decided that Ben should not be off work for the month of December as was this considered, "prime time." She didn't honor Ben's long-time agreement. I will not write about what happened because it is personal information. I will tell you that Ben went through a lot of channels with many challenges, but he got his days back until he retired.

"Party on Ben."

Health care at the U.S. Department of Veteran Affairs, which governs all federal veteran's hospitals, is the province of the cabinet agency's chief nursing officer. From 1980 to 1992, Vernice Ferguson, an African American held this position. While attending a nursing convention in Las Vegas, Nevada, I had the pleasure of meeting Ms. Ferguson, who was a guest speaker. I saw her standing alone in the foyer, and I was brave enough to go over to her, and introduce myself, and I told her that I worked for the Los Angeles VA. I found her to be warm and welcoming. Ms. Ferguson was interested in what I had to say about working for the VA. We talked for a few minutes and in parting, she asked me to give her greetings to the employees at the VA. Ms. Ferguson had an interesting and outstanding career. I highly recommend reading her story.

Over the years, as a registered nurse, I have worked with many outstanding nurses in all categories, RNs, LVNs, and CNA's. I have worked with nurses from around the world, Thailand, England, France, Mexico, the Caribbean Islands, Hatti, The Philippines, Korea, China, Canada, Korea, Germany, Africa, Cuba, and many other countries. It has been a wonderful experience to learn about their culture, food, religion, and family lifestyle from these nurses.

There are many nurses I will forever hold dear in my heart.

I have never considered myself a great nurse, just ordinary. However, I am thankful for the people I met and interacted with on this beautiful journey: the patients, the families, the doctors, and the nursing staff. The support staff including housekeeping, dietary, laundry workers, x-ray, lab workers, ambulance drivers, social service, PT, OT, and religious staff.

I salute all the nurses I have worked with during my career.

This book can't be complete without honoring the nursing faculty at Los Angeles Southwest College 1972-1974. I do not remember everyone's first name, but I remember their last name. I salute these very outstanding and distinguished educators.

Mrs. Helen Perkins, RN, Chairman
Mrs. Susan Bradshaw, RN, Medical-Surgical Nursing
Mrs. Tilly Chilk, RN, Medical-Surgical Nursing
Mrs. Beverly Dawson, RN, Medical-Surgical Nursing
Ms. Vivian Lott, RN, Psychiatric Nursing
Mrs. Friedland, RN, OB-GYN, Maternal Nursing, Pediatrics
Mrs. Reiner, RN, OB-GYN, Maternal Nursing, Pediatrics
Mrs. Julie Sykes, RN, Advanced Medical-Surgical Nursing

SECTION 3
DIFFICULT LESSONS

CHAPTER 10
Lesson of the Peach Orchard

LESSON #1:
*"Behold the wages you withheld from the workers
who harvested your fields are crying aloud, and the cries of the
harvesters have reached the ears of the Lord of hosts."*
—JAMES 5:4 TNAB

During the summer, when I was fifteen years old, a few of my friends and I decided to pick peaches to earn some money for school clothes. So, early in the morning before daylight, Reverend Reid would come to the Black neighborhoods to pick up Black people in his big open bed truck to take them to peach orchards in neighboring towns to pick peaches from sunup to sundown.

It was hard work because the heat of the sun and the fuzz from the peaches would cause severe itching of the skin, especially around the neck. Yet, we went along each day. The adults who came with us were kind and instructed us how to pick the peaches and how to stay cool in Georgia's burning heat.

We had gone a couple of times with no incidents or problems. Until one day, all hell broke loose. As a teenager, I had never witnessed such violent behavior. I was so terrified I could not speak or move. I was frozen. I now understand what happened on that hot summer day in that Georgia peach orchard.

We were all picking peaches when suddenly, a pick-up truck came roaring into the orchard. Dust was flying everywhere. The adults who had experienced this type of behavior knew what was about to happen. However, it was a terrifying experience for many of us teenagers.

An overweight white man, sporting a big "beer belly." with bloodshot, menacing eyes, came storming and cursing into the orchard. As an adult with more life experiences, now, I know that he was probably an alcoholic and a bigot because of his language. He called us a bunch of Black bastards and niggers.

I had never seen a person in such a rage. I had heard many stories about the Ku Klux Klan and the dreadful things they did to African American people but, I will never forget the look of rage and hate on that man's face. If looks could kill, we would all have been dead that day.

Part of our fear was that we all knew the story about the brutal lynching of Emmett Till. A young African American boy from Chicago, Illinois, visiting relatives, and his Uncle Moses Wright, a sharecropper in Money, Mississippi, for his summer vacation, was brutally murdered. Emmett had been helping to harvest the cotton crop.

On August 28, 1955, Emmett's killers threw his mutilated body into the Tallahatchie River after shooting him in the head. They accused him of flirting with or whistling to a 21-year-old white woman, Carolyn Bryant, a store owner. Emmett was only 14 years old. Carolyn Bryant reported to her husband that Emmett had disrespected her. Carolyn's husband, Roy Bryant, and J. W. Milam, Bryant's half-brother, abducted Till from his uncle's home and murdered him, based on hearsay.

There is so much written about his murder, more than I could ever write here. I urge all readers, especially African Americans, to read about this unfortunate tragic event in our bloody history here in The United States of America.

Years later, I was having a casual conversation with my husband, Marcus, and he told me he was among the marchers who marched in protest over the death of Emmett Till in Chicago, Illinois. I felt proud of my husband for standing up for injustice.

NOTABLY:
Emmett Till's original casket was donated to the Smithsonian National Museum of African American History and Culture in Washington, D.C.

We had been picking peaches all morning, and the owner ordered us out of his peach orchard and did not pay us for the work we had done that morning.

Reverend Reid, the person responsible for bringing us to the orchard, was a Black Christian minister. He was kind, soft-spoken, and a gentleman. He had just the right words to console us and get us out of this terrible situation.

This event happened when African Americans began to have sit-ins in the South. It was in the early days of the Civil Rights movement. Reverend Reid was a father, practiced non-violence, and he was well respected; adults and children in Eatonton held him in high regard. He was a strong and courageous man on that day.

Reverend Reid did not shout and demand our rights to be paid for our work. Instead, he told us to get onto the truck's bed. He said, "I will never bring my people to this orchard again. There are other orchards we can go to."

I remember one of my friends crying and saying, "I have a father. I am not a bastard." It was a painful lesson we learned that summer day. It was the most outward display of racial hate I have ever witnessed in my lifetime. It also taught us to go to school so we would not have to do this type of work, only to be cheated out of our wages and humiliated. We learned we could do better in life.

We were degraded and humiliated in the worse way, but I learned self-control. A person can be insulted terribly yet retain their pride and their dignity. A person does not have to fight back verbally or physically to win a battle. Just be still, and let the Lord fight your battle.

LESSON NUMBER 2:

"The getting of treasures by a lying tongue is a fleeting vapor and a snare of death"
—Proverbs 21:6 ESV

Life is full of lessons, some good and some not so good. Every lesson a person learns that helps shape their character is not always pleasant, but many of these lessons you will never forget. Some of these lessons can hurt deeply and be very painful such as Lesson Number 2 of the Peach Orchard.

I had two younger brothers, both now deceased, Larry and Paul. One summer, the three of us went to a peach orchard in a neighboring town to pick peaches.

The three of us picked lots of peaches. My two brothers could climb up into the trees while I carried the peaches and dumped them into the box. The procedure was to call out your assigned number and place your number on the box of peaches you picked. A young white boy, named Tim, kept the record. We were paid according to the number of boxes of peaches we picked each day. My brothers and I picked more peaches than anyone else in the peach orchard because we were young and fast.

I noticed two African American women sitting under the peach trees on two trips to the boxes. I assumed they were taking a break. However, I was a teenager, and it was not my business as to why these grown-ups were sitting under the trees and not working. I emptied my peaches, called out our number, and returned to pick more peaches.

78

I was minding my own business when a short time later, I was approached by Tim. He asked me where were the two boxes that I had just filled.

I remember vividly that that our number was 24. I pointed to the boxes I had just filled, but our number was not there. To my surprise, someone else's number was on the boxes. I was speechless. I did not know how to defend myself except to insist I had placed the peaches we had picked in those boxes.

Tim called the boss of the peach orchards. The boss said the two African American women sitting under the peach trees had reported us for calling out our number and not picking any peaches.

I was very shocked and in disbelief.

The boss told me and my brothers we were not to pick any more fruit and never return to the peach orchard. We had to sit down until time to go home when the truck came for us. My brothers and I were disgraced for cheating. To be lied on by African American adults was a hard lesson to accept.

I was hurt beyond words because we had worked so hard. But, to me, it was not about the loss of two boxes of peaches. It was the lie that they told on us.

They sat under the tree while we worked and stole our pay and integrity. I thought we would stick up for each other because we were Black—it was a harsh lesson to learn. I had not yet discovered the lesson of "Uncle Tom and Aunt Sally." But, the thoughts I have today are, *what did these two women do after they got us fired? And how many boxes of peaches did they pick?*

Living in a small town made it difficult to see these two women and contain my rage. But, as an adult, I know now these women lacked character. They were mothers of young children, and I went to school with a sibling of one of these women. Sitting in a classroom with a sibling and not saying what they did to us that past summer in the peach orchard was hard.

In contrast to these two women, many of the adults were helpful to us teenagers. I remember a kind man telling us to bring an old towel the next day, to put around our neck. This was to keep the peach fuzz from itching the neck and also act as a sweat rag. The adults told us to wear a straw hat, and to drink plenty of water. We did not know about sunscreen. Some adults would offer food to the other workers. These are the kind of adults I was familiar with.

I am sure many of these people wanted the best for us. Some would ask us how we were doing in school. I am sure they wanted to hear good things about us in the future. That is why it hurts so bad to be lied on. You see, I wanted *to be the dream and the hope of the slave*, as Maya Angelou states in her poem, "I Rise."

Sometimes in life it is hard to forgive and to forget. However, this was part of my growing up. I learned a valuable lesson, and I have been able to move on. In September 2021, a friend from Georgia told me many of these peach orchards no longer exist.

Today, I thank God for all that I have accomplished in my lifetime, so much that I don't focus on someone's lies and the stealing of a box of peaches worth fifty cents.

CHAPTER 11

Lost Dreams

A MIND IS A TERRIBLE THING TO WASTE

DREAM #1: NO CLOTHES TO WEAR

Somethings do not sink into our brains when we are growing up and maturing. After having life experiences, one can fully comprehend what happened years ago. Many people just let life happen. Some people float through life with no real direction or purpose. Sometimes this can occur because of the family structure, a lack of education, economic conditions, and racial inequality.

Statements such as these are true:

- Only the strong survive
- One must pull oneself by his bootstraps
- The prize goes to the fittest
- One must keep their eye on the prize

Some people will pull you down. I call them crabs, which will keep you from accomplishing your goals. Unfortunately, I know some of those people, and I've met plenty of these people in my lifetime.

When I was fifteen years old, I missed seeing one of my classmates at school. Then, one day I saw her at the store. I asked her why she was not at school. She told me she had quit school. I asked her, "Why?"

Usually, when a girl leaves school, she was pregnant. This classmate was not. But, she said, "I don't have any clothes to wear to school."

I was stunned.

I said, "Your older brother is working can't he buy you some clothes?" She said, "No."

I knew there were about six children in her family. "What about your parents?"

She said, "They can't help."

It was an unfortunate experience for me to see the hurt, shame, and pain in my classmate's eyes. I felt so helpless. I, too, was young, and I didn't have words of comfort or any solution to her dilemma. I had two parents, but I knew I had to look out for myself early. So, I learned how to use the resources available in my community. I picked peaches and cotton to earn money, worked at my aunt Roberta Café on Saturdays and Sundays, and worked at the Jordan Hospital during my junior year in high school.

I have encountered successful people who picked cotton, milked cows, fed hogs, and many other jobs. Today, many of these people live in lovely homes, drive nice cars, enjoy the finer things in life, and have money in the bank.

Years later, I heard this classmate moved from Eatonton, and later married and had children. As to the success of her children, I do not know their fate. I don't know if they graduated from high school, went to college, married, became good citizens, or ended up on the wrong side of life. Even today, when I think of her, it pains me. I wish my old classmate the best.

DREAM #2: THE PIANO

I went to school with a very annoying boy named Nick. The labels we used to put on boys with his problems were "mannish" and "fresh." He would pull girl's hair and tease them. As Nick got older, his behavior progressed to other things, and he would try to touch girls when they passed his desk. All the girls knew about him, and we learned to avoid him. Nick would say very inappropriate things, even in public as a teenager. He loved to tell off-color jokes about people. It was pretty embarrassing and hurtful to be the object of his jokes. I disliked him and avoided him as much as possible.

Eventually, everyone grows up. Years later, we were older and wiser when Nick and I had a civil conversation. He asked,

"Do you remember Mrs. Mayfield?"

I answered, "Yes, I do."

"I was so sorry I had to quit school to go to work. When we got to our new school, and Mrs. Mayfield came to teach music, I was interested in learning how to play the piano. I loved Mrs. Mayfield and her class. I'm so sorry I didn't get a chance to learn how to play the piano."

I was surprised to hear this coming from Nick. Mrs. Mayfield was a trained musician. She read and could play all types of jazz, classical and spiritual music. She even taught us about Bach and Beethoven.

We learned the scales. We learned about different types of music. We often could hear Mrs. Mayfield playing the piano when she didn't have a class. I suppose she was practicing as she did not have a piano where she lived; Mrs. Mayfield was from out of town. It was quite a privilege having a teacher as talented as Mrs. Mayfield in our little African American school.

Nick is a hard worker and has accomplished a lot without a high school diploma. He has a family, owns property, and is a good citizen in his community. But who knows what Nick could have become if he had learned to play the piano?

"A mind is a terrible thing to waste."

—ARTHUR FLETCHER,
FORMER HEAD OF THE
UNITED NEGRO COLLEGE FUND

CHAPTER 12
Believe What Children Tell You

MARIJUANA GROWING IN MY BACKYARD

Children often say things to adults that adults disregard. In some instances, children have told their parents about the abuse, and children are told that it was their fault, or that they encouraged the wrongful act.

When I lived in Los Angeles, a married man who lived on our street allegedly harassed a teenage girl who was a foster child. The girl told her foster father, and he visited the married man. When the married man learned that some of the neighbors and his wife knew about his inappropriate behavior, he stopped harassing the teenager. This kind of harassment is why we need to listen to our children.

Early one school morning, "Big Melody" rang my doorbell. She said, "Mrs. Lowe, I am here to let you know your tenant, Billy, is growing marijuana in your backyard."

I was astonished, but I asked her how did she know?

She said, "Everybody on the street, but you know what is going on . . . go take a look."

I had known "Big Melody" for most of her life; her family lived on our street before we moved there. So therefore, I knew her parents, grandparents, siblings, and extended family members. I had never heard anything negative about her; therefore, I had no reason not to believe her.

I had chosen the name Melody for my daughter before I knew "Big Melody." So, my daughter became known as "Little Melody."

Big Melody was a student at St. Michaels Catholic School, our local parish, about a mile from our home. Big Melody, her siblings, and my children often took the city bus to Sunday Mass. It reminded me of my childhood when I walked to church with my cousins and the neighborhood children back in Georgia. The children were always well-behaved, and never had any bad reports on their trips to and from church. Therefore, knowing her family and her background, I believed her about Billy was growing marijuana in my backyard.

I studied marijuana and other plant-based drugs in school, such as the poppy plant. Therefore, I knew how to identify a marijuana plant. I pulled out an old textbook from school and searched for pictures of what was growing in my yard. They matched.

I seldom went into our backyard; my husband did the gardening. I discovered Billy had very cleverly planted his marijuana plants among the tropical plants. I have never smoked marijuana; however, I know what "pot" smelled like because, back in the day, people would smoke pot in public parks. Knowing that pot was growing in my backyard terrified me.

As a registered nurse, the possibility of losing my nursing license that I had struggled so hard to get, it was frightening. Plus, I feared going to jail. Who would believe that I didn't know what was growing in my backyard? I was afraid of losing my children for being an unfit mother and being embarrassed by my church and community. I could envision the newspaper headline, "Nurse Growing Marijuana in Her Backyard." What would my nursing classmates and instructors think of me? I would be a disgrace. So many thoughts raced through my mind. What would my family, especially my parents, think?

I refused to call the Los Angeles Police Department because I felt they might blow it out of proportion due to the area where I lived. At that time, you could lose your property if illegal drugs were found on it. My husband was at work when I received this information. I felt I had to act quickly. The first person that came to mind was Mr. Levester, who did our income taxes. I knew I could count on the advice of a certified public accountant, a real estate broker, and a property owner.

Mr. Levester knew exactly what to do. He said, "Go to the stationery store, buy a 'Notice to Quit' form. Fill it out and send it to your tenant by certified mail, so he must sign for it. Then, give him a date to remove the plants and vacate your property. If he doesn't cooperate, then report him to the police. Meanwhile, don't talk with the tenant about this matter. Call me again if you need me." It was divine help.

I went right away to the stationery store, purchased the form, filled it out, and mailed it to Billy. During that time, Office Depot was not located in the South Central Los Angeles area. As soon as he received the form, he came looking for me. Billy was likable; I had never witnessed him angry or violent. He was always cheerful and easygoing.

He said, "My plants are not ready to be pulled up; they can't be smoked."

"I am so sorry about that, but you know I am a nurse, and I have young children. So, you and your plants both must go. If you don't abide by the notice, I will call the police."

I still find it amazing how much liberty people will take with other people's property. It's hard to imagine people doing such things as planting illegal plants and moving other people onto the property without notifying the owners. Sometimes tenants will reconnect utilities when they have been shut off for non-payment, bring animals onto the property without the owner's consent, damage and destroy the property, and so much more.

I know there are good tenants who pay their rent on time and don't willfully damage and destroy property. They don't move in extra people or animals into the property, and they take care of the property as if it was their own. However, as a landlord, I've had some unpleasant experiences with several tenants.

While writing this story, I pondered how Big Melody had learned about the marijuana plants growing in my backyard and how she was confident enough to report it to me. I am not sure if she told her parents, grandparents, or a teacher. I never found out how she had the courage to report it to me. However, I am grateful to Big Melody. She saved me a lot of trouble, and I am glad I listened to her.

Big Melody graduated from high school, and after graduation, she went to school to study culinary arts. The last thing I heard about her was that she had become a chef.

I consulted with my daughter about what she remembered about this incident. At the time, my daughter was the youngest child in the bunch. I was not sure she would remember this incident; however, she remembered quite a bit.

"Of course, I remember Billy. He was my favorite tenant. He had a cool manner about him. He respected us. He always talked to us kids. He was the one growing the marijuana in the backyard."

It confirmed my evaluation that Billy was an easy-going and kind person. I asked her how Big Melody knew about was in our backyard.

She said, "Don't you remember, we had a basketball hoop in our backyard and kids came over to play with us?"

She explained, "One day, we ran around the rear back house and saw the marijuana plants. Big Melody was the oldest and said she knew what they were, that she would tell you and Dad."

I further corroborated my daughter's account of the incident with my son who is older. He remembered the incident too, and his version was the same as my daughter's. Both of my children thought Billy pulled the wool over our eyes. Children know more than we give them credit for knowing.

I must have scared Billy because he pulled up the plants and moved. When he moved, he was behind in his rent, and I never recovered the rent money. However, it was okay.

The lesson of this: Keep the lines of communication open with young people. I remember my daughter telling me when she was young. "Mom, I am reporting everything to you; now, when something happens, don't say I didn't tell you."

I often think of this conversation and wonder, where did she learn that? I still remember the look of innocence on her little face.

Out of the mouth of babes!

CHAPTER 13
Somewhere a Child Is Waiting

COCOA

To relieve the stress of working as a nurse, I enjoyed taking short trips. Some years ago, I went on a day bus trip. There were about three or four people already on the bus when I arrived. My feet were aching, and I was tired from walking, so I took my seat. I had hoped to catch a little nap. However, shortly after I sat down, a well-dressed woman, about fifty years old, approached me.

She said, "Hello, my name is Cocoa."

I wondered what she wanted.

I said, "Hello."

At first, I thought she wanted to talk about her day's events. I remembered she was wearing a nice turquoise pantsuit. I also noticed her hair, which was very long and appeared to be dyed a warm brown color.

I had not seen her before, and I didn't know if she was alone or came with someone on the trip.

Her next question surprised me. "Do you have any children?"

"Yes," I replied. " I have two children."

At this time, both of my children were grown, and I had grandchildren.

I wondered, *Where this was going? What does this woman want?*

I was a stranger, and we would probably never see each other again. Perhaps, this was why she felt highly comfortable sharing the next part of her life story with me; even though there were others on the bus that could easily hear our conversation.

However, Cocoa was determined to tell me her story.

Over the years, I have had several people confide in me with highly personal things about themselves during my lifetime. These conversations would occur while standing in a line at the bank, the mall, the airport, the grocery store, the car wash, the fish market, the post office, or other random places. I have learned a lot about people in just a few short minutes. I think my quiet, unassuming appearance is what prompts many people to approach me. I have often wondered if I have gullible, fool, stupid, country, or other adjectives tattooed on my forehead. I am not sure many of these stories are factual; however, some are very memorable.

I was not prepared for her following words. Her story went like this:

While in college, she became pregnant before marriage. She did not want her parents to know, so she chose to have an illegal abortion. This was before Roe v. Wade, the January 22, 1973, Supreme Court decision that made abortions legal in the United States.

Cocoa was lucky she did not die. She graduated from college, and after graduation, she obtained a high-paying position and had a successful career. A few years after graduating from college, she met and married a wonderful man. With their combined salaries, they had a secure and comfortable life. Cocoa and her husband could have easily provided for one or two children. To her dismay, Cocoa could not conceive another child, although she didn't share the reason. I'm not sure if her body had been traumatized by the abortion or if her husband suffered from a medical condition that prevented conception. There are situations where a woman had children and a man had children, but when together they could not produce a child.

I don't know what triggered her to share this with me. I could tell by the look on her face and the pain in her voice she was hurting. I prayed silently, "Lord, why did you put this woman before me at this time?" Please tell me what to say to her."

I was exhausted from the day's events, and I was not in a pleasant mood. I did not want to be bothered by this woman. It was raining, and I had to walk to the bus—I was cold and wet. I just wanted to relax; however, I was frustrated because I had forgotten my little blanket that I would bring on bus trips.

Cocoa went on to tell me that her husband had recently died, and she was all alone. She said they had paid for their home, and she had a comfortable life. I asked her why she and her husband did not adopt or take in a foster child. I said, "It is always advertised that so many minority children, especially African Americans, need foster care, and African American children are seldom adopted."

She said, "My husband said if he could not be a natural father, he did not want to raise another man's child. He could not bear to raise a child that was not his."

My advice to her was, "You are now a widow and all alone; what is preventing you from adopting a child or becoming a foster mother?"

Cocoa looked at me in stunned amazement and said, "You know I have never thought about that. Thank you, I will consider it." Cocoa had a big smile on her face, and without another word, she returned to her seat.

I never saw her again, and I would not recognize her if I were to see her. I wish her all the best in life. I pray she found peace, and I hope she found that beautiful and special child to share her life with.

"A child is still waiting."

ROE VS. WADE UPDATE

Early in February 2022, a draft of a major opinion written by Supreme Court Justice Samuel Alito that would strike down Roe V. Wade leaked to the press.

This draft was obtained and published by Politico. The authenticity of the document has been confirmed by the Supreme Court. The leaking of this document is shocking that such a confidential document could be leaked.

June 24, 2022, the Supreme Court overturned Roe vs. Wade. Immediately, there were demonstrations and lawsuits filed to challenge this decision. However, we should be vigilant and watch the news and medical report to see how women are being affected by this decision.

One definition of abortion is preventing a human being the right to experience life as we know it.

The sixth commandment states: Thou shall not kill.

In Nursing One, it was emphasized over and over again to never be judgmental of others. Nurses are trained to keep their personal opinions to themselves. Whenever nurses are working with patients, they are to show compassion and be supportive of the patient's needs, educate them but not chastise them.

Pope Francis saw how women had suffered from the pain of having an abortion. In November 2016, the pope granted Roman Catholic priests the power to give absolution to women who had an abortion. This is known as the "Year of Mercy."

Jesus spoke these words:

"Amen, I say to you, whatever you bind on earth shall be bound in heaven, and whatever you lose on earth shall be loosed in heaven"
—MATHEWS 18:18 (NAB)

MY REFLECTION

1. Over many centuries, many women have died as a result of illegal abortions, due to infection, bleeding, puncture wounds etc.

2. As a result of unsafe and illegal many women bodies have been damaged for life, many never to be able to conceive again.

3. Many women are never able to have a "normal" relationship with a man again after an abortion.

4. Many women suffer mental illness, such as depression, because of abortion. It has been reported men can be greatly affected by abortion as well.

5. Abortion should never be used as birth control.

I am thinking of Cocoa: If she had had a legal abortion, would she be able to have a child, and would she be in less mental anguish? These are questions I will never know the answer to. However, as we approach the overturning of Roe vs. Wade, we should watch the medical reports and see how women are affected by this decision.

As with many of my stories, you readers must reach your own conclusions.

CHAPTER 14

George

LOVE IS COLOR BLIND

One afternoon, I walked into a patient's room for the first time. The patient was in bed. He greeted me with, "Hello, Sister."

I was confused. I thought someone was walking behind me. The patient was a middle-aged white male named George. He had a round or "moon face," with blond, thin hair. Sitting in a chair at his bedside was a woman. She was attractive, with thick jet black, naturally curly hair. She was later identified as his wife, Christie.

George reacted to my puzzled look with another bolt out of nowhere. "From the first moment I saw you outside of my room, I felt like you are my sister, and I fell in love with you," he said.

I thought, *What a strange thing to say to a black nurse.*

Sometimes medications make patients hallucinate. So, I just tried to ignore what he just said and went on with my job. But each time I encountered George; he would always tell me how much he loved me. His wife and two sons visited him every day. He would constantly say these things in front of his family, and he always called me "Sister."

After a few days, I ceased to feel embarrassed.

George and Christie had two sons; both had jet-black hair like their mother. One son had very thin hair, like George and, he also had his father's moon-shaped face. The other son had thick natural black curly hair, like their mother, and had her fine features and her quiet personality.

George was in a terminal state. One afternoon he told me that his sister from Mississippi was coming the next day to visit him; he asked if I would be working.

"Yes, I will be here."

"Good . . . I want you to meet Carolyn."

The next day I went into his room to meet Carolyn. Both Christie and Carolyn were at George's bedside.

He said, "Carolyn, this is the sister I told you about. I don't know why I love her, but I do. I am married, and she is married, too. So, it is not a sexual thing. But the very first time I saw her, I fell in love with her."

Carolyn was friendly, and she laughed loudly and smiled a lot. She and George had similar personalities, thin blond hair, and their skin tone was the same reddish color. Carolyn visited with George for several days. While visiting George, Carolyn smiled often and was always upbeat. All of George's family members were delightful people. They never complained about the care George was receiving. They were never demanding. Maybe this was because he was such a friendly person.

As time went by, I learned not to be offended, by George's words. I don't think any of his family was offended either. No one ever challenged George on what he said to me.

Doctors told George he didn't have much longer to live earlier in the day.

After visiting hours and his family had gone home, George ran away. It happened on a rainy Sunday night. We looked all over the hospital and couldn't find him. Finally, we had to notify his wife, call security, and we paged George repeatedly over the hospital speaker. We were afraid he would have tried to harm himself.

Shortly, after midnight security returned George to us, safe and unharmed. He said he had taken the elevator down to the basement and got confused about getting back to the elevator. So, he had been wandering about down there when security found him.

I came on duty some days later, and the shift report said George was dying. I went in to see him for the last time. George was already unresponsive; his beloved wife was at his bedside. So often, when a person passes away in the hospital, the family wants a chance to say a final goodbye before their loved one is taken to the mortuary. Nurses must know how to prepare the patient and family for this journey. The person must be bathed, put on a clean gown, and groomed. The bed linen should be changed, and the room should be tidy and orderly.

Two of our best CNAs, were on duty with me. They were mature women and knew how to give support to a grieving family. I felt very honored to be there to help take care of Christie. I was happy I was there with George as she gave her final goodbye. Christie was such a kind person and loving wife, always calm and pleasant to talk to.

Watching the two CNAs escort Christie in for her goodbye was like watching something very holy and moving. It is hard to describe. It was one of the feelings a nurse happens to experience only once in their career.

Later that evening, we were able to talk about the experience. We felt we had done our best as we worked closely with the family. Christie knew us, and we had been there for her. She did not break down but was strong as she left the hospital, escorted by her sons.

George left us very peacefully. I often think of him. I don't know why God allowed George and me to have this experience. Today, I wish I had been less stiff, more lighthearted, and more accepting of his open display of affection toward me. Maybe, we both needed something. I still ask why?

"So, faith, hope, love remains, these three.
but the greatest of these is LOVE."
—1 CORINTHIANS 13:13

CHAPTER 15
Social Graces

*"... I was a stranger
and you welcomed me..."*

Hospitality is a lost art in today's fast-paced society. People today prefer paper plates, plastic utensils, plastic tablecloths, and plastic cups to fine china, linen, silverware, and crystal stemware.

There was a time when entertaining; the host showed great pride in displaying their fine china, silverware, crystal stemware, and table linen. The table presentation was just as important as the presentation of the food.

December 1981, I found a flyer in my mailbox, and it read, "You are invited to dessert and coffee at our house." The invitation gave a name, a date, a time, and an address. We had lived in Los Angeles for more than twenty years before moving to the San Fernando Valley, approximately 25 miles North of Los Angeles. People in Los Angeles were not as friendly as in Georgia. I had never received an invitation to a stranger's home. Therefore, I was extremely curious to visit our neighbor, the Taylor's home. They lived around the corner on the next street, they too were new to the neighborhood.

Back then, Lake View Terrace was rural. There were lots of empty spaces around us. The Lake View Terrace, Sunland, and Tujunga areas were considered "horse country." We had moved into a new development, and we did not know anyone who lived in the Valley. My husband worked in Burbank, eight miles away, which prompted us to move into this community.

We looked forward to this adventure and to meeting our new neighbors. I had discussed the flyer with my husband, and we decided to see what it was all about. At the time, our daughter, Melody, was 13 years old, so we took her along, which turned out to be a great decision.

Happy Kwanzaa

Blessed Las Posadas

Merry Christmas

Happy Hanukkah

It's time for good neighbors to share in the Spirits of

TEE HOLIDAYS!

Please join us for

SPIRITS, DESSERTS, AND COFFEE

On

Tuesday Evening,

December 21, 1981

7:00 p.m.

11405 Sunburst St.

THE FAMILY IS INVITED!

From

THE TAYLOR'S

JAMES, JANIE, ROBERT, BRUCE

Upon entering the host's home, we were welcomed by a small petite woman who was both vivacious and soft-spoken. She introduced herself as Janie and her husband's name was James. Janie is a very refined Southern lady. She made us feel comfortable and welcomed us into her lovely home. Janie, too, is a part of the Great Migration, she came from Tennessee to California.

Janie had an awesome display of several desserts. I had never seen such a display in a home, only in restaurant settings. She must have been baking for days, I thought. All was so delicious. Janie served punch and coffee to compliment her wonderful desserts. Janie's home was beautifully decorated for the holiday season. It was a new, impressive and unforgettable experience for all of us.

We learned Janie was a school principal. She and Melody took to each other right away. Over the years, we have remained friends. Melody was involved in a highly rated drama program in the Valley at the time. Her school always brought home the prizes. Much of the school's drama program success was credited to a dedicated husband-and-wife team.

Janie would often take off from her job to see my daughter perform, that is how much she loved children and how involved she was with what they were doing. I wish I could have met Janie when my children were younger. Over the years, Janie and Melody have bonded and have a special relationship. Janie was the moderator of "Jumping the Broom" at Melody's wedding. She has continued to support Melody through the birth of her children, their graduations, and other occasions.

Being friends with Janie made me try to do my best in many areas of my personal life. I tried to keep my home in order, be careful of how I spoke, improve my English. I began to watch the news to keep up with the world's current events, especially what was going on in my community. Janie reminds me of my dear Auntie and Mr. W. N. McGlockton. It has been wonderful having Janie as a neighbor and a friend. Our friendship exists even today. I know I can call on her, and she can always call on me.

Janie has one son. She told me she had wanted more children, especially a daughter, but she didn't. Janie expressed how she had taken care of her body to have more children, but she only had one child. She gives lots of her love to her nieces, nephews, students, friends, and many other people. She is a people person and proud to work in the nursery at her church.

Over the years, I learned how generous she can be. I went to her home one Christmas holiday. I was amazed, her living room was overflowing with presents. Most of these presents were for her school staff. Janie bought and wrapped present to everyone that worked at her school from the teachers to the janitorial staff.

Unbelievable!

Though Janie was a principal, she was not a rich woman. I asked Janie how could she afford all these presents?

She said, "I start early. I catch sales and I recycle newspapers, and cans to get extra money, I know what I must do."

This was a great lesson for me. I, too, started to shop for bargains, shop for sales, use coupons, use my credit card "cash back" perks to be able to provide gifts for others. In these early days, my husband and I even started to recycle cans and bottles. I still shop for sales. I feel good when I know I have gotten a great bargain.

Shopping and matching each gift with a particular person takes a lot of time. You must have an insight into the personality each person. I realized, that to be able to give this many presents, it takes lots of energy to wrap and label present as well. It means giving up much of home or free time. Also, it takes love to do this year after year. I don't think many people, even I, would take on this huge project every Christmas for years.

Janie uses common sense. When my brother died, she brought eggs, bacon, and orange juice. She said," You will have people in your house, here is something easy that anyone can fix."

I never would have thought of taking breakfast food to someone, most people bring a card or a plant.

SPECIAL NOTE

Janie and James waited many years for a grandchild. A few years ago, God blessed them with a beautiful granddaughter. She finally got her little girl. Good things come to those who wait.

Forty years later, I am glad we accepted that invitation for dessert and coffee. I don't think I can match Janie's generosity, but I try to be consistently thoughtful and as generous as I can.

All the BEST, James and Janie!
"I was a stranger and you welcomed me"

CHAPTER 16
Integrity

"LET YOUR WORD BE YOUR BOND."

I was eighteen years old when I met my grandmother's youngest sister for the first time. My great aunt's given name is Ruth. Some years later she changed her name to Mamie Ruth, she was known as Mamie or Aunt Mamie. Aunt Mamie, as I called her was a very extroverted woman. She was a tall impressive African American woman, and always impeccably dressed. On the day I first met her, it was a Sunday and she had just come from church. I remember she was wearing a black suit, a big black hat, black shoes, and stockings.

She had come to California from Georgia with a white family. Aunt Mamie had worked as a domestic worker for many years and had worked for some very rich and famous people in Hollywood and Beverly Hills, California. I am sure most people would recognize their names.

Aunt Mamie lost all ties with her family in Georgia when she came to California. However, she did have some nieces and their families living in Los Angeles. I asked her why she would not go to Georgia. She told me a story of how her only child, a girl, had tragically died in a fire in Georgia and she could never bear to go home again. Whenever, a relative died in Georgia, Aunt Mamie would tell her family members, "I will help pay your fare, but I am not going."

I am not sure of Aunt Mamie's education level, but because of working for the type of people she worked for and the amount of traveling she did with her employers, she had a wealth of knowledge

Somewhere along the way, she lost her southern accent. Auntie spoke very proper English. This is what happens when you associate with educated and wealthy people.

Aunt Mamie had traveled to many cities in the United States, but she had also traveled aboard. Egypt was one of the places she told me she had visited and had seen the great pyramids and rode on a camel.

Even when Aunt Mamie was very advanced in age, she continued to enjoy life. She loved all types of plants and flowers and had both potted plants as well yard plants and enjoyed watering and caring for her plants. Aunt Mamie was a great fan of horse racing, she followed the career of jockey Bill Shoemaker to see if he would break the record of Johnny Longden. She also enjoyed going to Las Vegas whenever someone would take her. Most of the time Aunt Mamie was very happy and loved to tease people. She was the closest I had to a grandmother.

I was blessed to have met Aunt Mamie and I remember so much of what she told me. She lived in my rental house for about four years before she died. As with many things I am not sure of how old Aunt Mamie was because of poor recordkeeping. My aunt Louella said she was sure Aunt Mamie lived to be over one hundred years old.

Aunt Mamie, faithfully read her Bible and her church's newsletter. She was constantly quoting scripture from the Bible. Her favorite quote was "Let your word be your bond." Aunt Mamie believed in being on time for all her appointments, paying her bills on time and doing what she said she had promised to do. Whenever, I was to drive her some place, she was always ready before time. These were the some of the traits she instilled in me, my children, and my husband. Aunt Mamie did not hesitate to correct or instruct anyone.

My dream was to be a registered nurse, and I achieved my dream. The hallmark of a registered nurse is integrity. The very life of another human being relies on the integrity of the registered nurse.

Registered nurses are exposed to the very personal side of a person. They perform all types of invasive procedures on patients, and are not to laugh, ridicule, make a joke about anything they experience while in their professional care of duty. The doctor is the head of the medical team, but it is the registered nurse that is the eyes and ears of the doctor. Hospitals entrust the narcotics keys to the licensed nurse, and they expect every narcotic to be always accounted for.

One morning, while on duty at the hospital where I worked, a nurse reported she dropped a narcotic pill onto the floor, and she could not find it. She asked the other staff to help her look for the pill. The staff searched for about fifteen minutes, but no one could find the pill. We searched with flashlights and some of the staff got down on their hands and knees looking for the pill. The nursing supervisor had to write a report. No one got in trouble. No one suspected the nurse of lying. About a month later, the housekeeper was mopping the floor in the medicine room, and he found the missing pill. No one could explain why and how this happened.

However, people will test our integrity many times. In a previous chapter, "Lessons of the Peach Orchard," I wrote that my two younger brothers and I were accused of calling our number and not picking any peaches. It was a very painful thing that happened to us. We learned about lying by adults.

Forty-five years after the peach orchard incident my integrity was questioned. I was a very seasoned nurse when this event occurred. Early in my shift, I noticed the nursing supervisor reading one of my assigned patient's charts. I know nursing supervisors have many reasons to read patient's chart. Perhapsk a doctor or family member had made a complaint, maybe there has been an incident that could have happened on another shift, an unusual lab report, or the patient needs to be transferred to another level of care, or many other reasons. I had just come on duty, and I had never taken care of this patient. However, I was not concerned.

When I came into the nursing station, the nursing supervisor approached me and asked, "Do you have a flashlight?'

I said, "Yes"

"Where is it?'

"In my pocket."

"May I see it?'

"Sure." I showed her my flashlight. "Do you want to borrow it?'

"No, I just wanted to see if you have one."

I understood right away why she wanted to see my flashlight. At this particular hospital, at the beginning of each shift, the registered nurse must perform a full assessment on each assigned patient. The assessment was from head to toe.

1. Check the pupils of the eyes—a flashlight is required.
2. Check breath sounds—a stethoscope is required.
3. Check for bowel sounds—A stethoscope is required.
4. Apical pulse—a watch with a second hand is required.
5. Radial pulses—a watch with a second hand is required.
6. Pedal pulses—check for presence of pulse, check warmth and color of extremity.
7. O2 saturation—a pulse oximetry is required.
8. Foot and leg strength—check for presence of the extremity, movement, and warmth, as the patient's could be an amputee.

The nursing supervisor wanted to see if I had falsified a patients record by not having the proper equipment. I knew my integrity was being tested. I knew a nurse can be fired for such an infraction of duty, and the supervisory staff observe and evaluate all nurses, and they know the character of all the nurses. Sometime later, this same nursing supervisor told me many of the patients had written very favorable evaluations of the care they had received from me. The hospital sends surveys to patients after they have been discharged from the hospital.

I will admit I have not always acted with integrity in many situations. I do not profess to be "Miss Goody Two Shoes." I remember one such incident when I received too much change from a cashier, and I kept it thinking, "this is my lucky day." I am guilty of gossiping and lying, however, I am trying to avoid theses vices in my older day.

I look for other alternative things to say instead of lying when asked questions I don't want to answer. For example, when confronted by a street beggar and I don't want to give him my money for personal reasons, I say, "I choose not to give you my money." That's what I say instead of telling them, "No, I don't have any money," or "I see you smoking," or "I see your can of beer." I try not to insult the beggar by telling them to get a job. I try not to judge the person begging me.

One of my friends told me she found $250.00 cash in a supermarket. It was near Christmas, and she kept it. I asked her had she talked with the store manager to see if someone had reported losing the money. She said, "No, he would probably have kept it himself. There is an old saying—loser's weepers, finder's keepers."

Her Christmas dinner consisted of big crab legs, steak and other expensive foods and drinks. Could the money had been someone's rent money, car payment, childcare payment or money for Christmas presents?

Since 2021, the United States of America is in a big crisis because of the "Big Lie"—that Donald J. Trump won the November election by a landslide. This lie has caused many problems that affect all the people of the United States of America. January 6, 2021, known as the attack on the Capitol in Washington, D.C., will always be remembered as shocking, unbelievable, a disgrace in America's history. The graphic images will never be erased. Many people will forever have a criminal record, many of these people had been law bidding citizens, many were professional people. Many of these people were simply mislead.

Some of the results of the January 6, 2021, event:
1. Death—10 total
2. Injuries—150 Capital Police officers—an unknown number of civilians
3. Property damage—approximate 1.5 million dollars
4. Court costs—unknown
5. Cost to incarcerate participants—unknown
6. Loss of American freedom—unknown
7. Fear, anxiety, sadness—cannot be measured
8. Mistrust of the American Voting Systems
9. Damage to the economy—unknown
10. Invasion of government private spaces
11. Damage to loss and of the American democracy
12. America was disgraced before the entire world

On October 18, 2021, Colin Powell, a great American died. During his lifetime, he had to endure a stain on his stellar reputation. This situation had to do with faulty intelligence used to justify the United Stated entering a war with Iraq. Colin Powell said, "I didn't lie. I did not know it was not true. I was the Secretary of State, not the director of intelligence." He said this would always leave an indelible stain. He spent many years working to rebuild his reputation. On his death, he was one of the most respected men in America.

EVERYDAY INTEGRITY:

1. Always speak the truth, no matter how painful or how uncomfortable it may be.
2. Do not gossip or speak badly about others.
3. Do not allow others to teach you how to cheat. For example, on your income taxes.
4. Refrain from swearing and cursing.
5. Develop a solid work ethic, do not waste time on your job. Today, the cell phone is a great time stealer on the job. Do not steal from your job. Be on time, give a day's work for a day's pay. Do not be a complainer.
6. Be kind, greet every stranger.
7. Be courteous to others.
8. Practice "Random Acts of Kindness," it is surprising what a little act of kindness can affect a person. For example: when you are in a store, allow a person with a small order to go ahead of you, if you have a large order. Place the divider on the conveyor belt to separate your order from the next person, it will help eliminate confusion for the cashier.
9. Apologize when you have offended someone.

CONCLUSION:

The lesson here is it's always best to tell the truth even when it is uncomfortable and painful. We must conduct ourselves with honesty and integrity in public and in private. What we do in the dark can be brought to light. However, there is no human being without blemishes or stains.

> *"Truthful lips will be established forever.*
> *But a lying tongue is (credited) only for a moment"*
> —PROVERBS 12-19 9 (AMP)

CHAPTER 17
Marriage

"FOR BETTER OR FOR WORSE"
A TALE OF THREE WIVES
(SHEILA, JANICE, AND ANGIE)

SHEILA

"For better or for worse, for richer or for poorer,
in sickness or in health, til death do us part."

The traditional wedding vows went something like the above sentence. The vows include the phrase, "honor and obey." Many brides did not like the word "obey." Today, couples select to write their vows. Ten years ago, I attended a wedding and was surprised to learn that the bride's father wasn't going to be "giving her away." I asked why, and was told you cannot give a person away; they're not property. Even though some of the wedding traditions have changed, the commitment to both the husband and wife should not change. The couple makes a commitment to love, honor, support, and be there for each other.

I met John as a patient. He was a certified public accountant who suffered from paraplegia. I cannot remember why John had paraplegia. John and his wife, Sheila, lived in a lovely and upscale community near the Pacific Ocean.

John told me he had worked very long hours to provide his beloved wife with all the luxuries she desired, a beautiful home, a nice car, expensive clothes, and she did not have to work. He often expressed to me how beautiful Sheila was and how much he loved her. John talked so much about Sheila, I felt as if I knew her. I had never seen her visit him, but she could have come when I was off. However, I was anxious to meet her.

I spent many hours performing his wound care; therefore, we spent lots of time together. He had sat for so many hours in his wheelchair that he developed a severe sore that was so deep, you could see his bone. He required extensive wound care such as debriding, packing, whirlpool treatment, constant turning, a special mattress, good hygiene, good nutrition, hydration, and pain management. Toward the end of his admission, John required mental health intervention.

During that time, it was a common practice to keep patients like John on a medical ward for an extended period of time. Today, these patients are stabilized then transferred to sub-acute, rehabilitation or a skilled nursing home.

One day, the head nurse told me that John's wife, Shelia, was coming the next day around 11 a.m. to learn how to care for John's wound at home. Wound care was the main part of John's discharge planning. The head nurse had ordered all the necessary supplies to send home. I was to make sure the supplies were on the ward before Sheila arrived. We were to teach Sheila and observe her changing John's dressing several times before sending him home.

Sheila arrived on time. She was stunningly beautiful, well dressed, and soft-spoken, a real lady, just as he described. I escorted Sheila into John's room. He was beaming from ear to ear, so happy to see his Sheila. I politely explained to Sheila what we were going to do.

I removed the outer dressing, and as I was beginning to remove the packing, Sheila said, "I can't do this. I can't take care of him. He will have to go to a nursing home." Sheila's beautiful face crumbled. It was a terrible scene. She ran out of the hospital and did not return that day. John was devasted and had a severe breakdown.

In the next few days, John required lots of supportive care from the medical and nursing staff, social service, mental health, the wound care nurse educator, and clergy. It was a sad situation to see and hear John cry. John was transferred to a nursing home.

I don't know if John and Sheila ever got back together again.

"What becomes of a broken heart?"

JANICE

"A Virtuous Woman"

It was December 23, the head nurse told me to prepare for Mr. Brown to go home for that day, at 2 p.m., until January 2.

A pass is granted to a patient by a doctor to leave the hospital for a specific amount of time and go to a specific place. Shortly after I started working at this facility, this practice stopped. A new administrator decided this was not a good practice. It was also baffling following to me for a patient to be in the hospital for five days and be allowed to go out on pass for the weekend. In a staff meeting, we were told when patients are not in the hospital it affected the budget.

Mr. Brown was totally dependent on someone for all his daily care, although he was alert and could talk. He had a foley catheter, wore a diaper, and had a feeding tube. As before, the head nurse ordered all the supplies he would need for home, and I made sure the supplies would be on the ward before the ambulance came for him.

We had Mr. Brown ready for the ambulance to pick him up. Around 1:30 p.m., a middle-aged woman arrived on the ward.

She introduced herself to me as Mrs. Brown. We, the staff, had no idea she was coming. She said she wanted to be there when the ambulance came for her husband. By her appearance, I assumed she was a professional woman. Mrs. Brown wore a business suit and high-heeled shoes and carried an expensive name-brand purse; she was neatly groomed, and her makeup and hair were all in order. Mrs. Brown was friendly, likable, and open and had a pleasant attitude.

I was very curious how Mrs. Brown would care for him, especially the number of days he would be home and his condition. Even though, I did not want to insult Mrs. Brown, I knew I had to ask the question. As tactfully as I could, I said, "Mr. Brown requires a lot of care."

"Yes, dear, I know, but it's Christmas. He is my husband, and I want him home with the family for Christmas."

Then I asked, "Can you manage?"

Mrs. Brown looked me directly in the eye, and with much confidence, said, "Don't worry, I have hired people to help me take care of my husband."

I could only look at Mrs. Brown with amazement and admiration.

On January 2, he returned in good shape as Mrs. Brown had promised. There were no bedsores, no signs of dehydration, neglect, or abuse. I was not on duty when he returned; however, when I did return to work, a young CNA was excited to tell me that Mr. Brown's wife and sons had accompanied Mr. Brown back to the hospital. I went in to see Mr. Brown and he proudly showed me his Christmas present, a navy-blue velour bathrobe, and he said he had a wonderful visit. I have worked in several hospitals; I have noticed patients that do not have anyone visit them. Mr. Brown was so blessed to have such a caring family.

During my conversations with Mr. Brown, I noticed how he lovingly said, "my wife," and the way his eyes would light up. By Mrs. Brown coming to be with her husband when he had to ride in the ambulance, speaks volumes.

Every Christmas, I fondly remember Mr. and Mrs. Brown. She will always be my role model for what a wife should be, in sickness and in health.

"Give her praise!"

ANGIE

"The Lady in Pink"

I enjoy going to casinos, my favorite activity is playing slot machines.

A neighbor encouraged me to try Bingo. I did, but Bingo was too slow for me. Over the years, I have tried almost every game including keno, blackjack, off track betting, and spinning the big wheel. Another reason I enjoy going is to casinos is that some have fancy seafood buffets. I love seafood, and I can eat crab legs, lobster, and shrimp, all at one price.

The typical bus ride is between two to five hours, depending on where I'm going. While traveling, I may do several things, such as sleep, work crossword puzzles, play video games, pray, meditate. Usually, praying and meditating leave my mind very refreshed. I have been able to solve many problems or reach a conclusion while riding the casino bus. Sometimes, it's difficult to do these activities because of my seatmate. Some seatmates want to talk. A few will go to sleep and snore, and a few will crowd my space. Some have offensive odors. I always shower, use deodorant, and use mouthwash when I know I must sit beside someone for a few hours.

I have met some very interesting people both on the bus and at the casino. I have had people confide in me and share all sorts of unbelievable stories. I'm not sure if they were always telling the truth.

One summer day, as I was waiting for the bus, a woman came up to me and asked, "Where did you buy your pants? They are very similar to mine."

I was wearing some white pants with sparkles on the pockets and sparkles going down the sides of the legs.

The lady turned around to show me her backside. Her pants were pink with sparkles on the pockets and sparkles going down the side of the legs. I told her I had ordered them from a catalog.

The very talkative and energetic lady introduced herself as Angie. When the bus arrived, she followed me onto the bus, sat

beside me and continued chatting. As we were riding along, we passed a large well-known company.

"That is where that old S.O.B. used to work," Angie said.

"What old S.O.B. are you talking about?

"My husband."

"Why did you call him a S.O.B.?"

"I am the mother of four boys. When my youngest son was a senior in high school, I was diagnosed with breast cancer, in both breasts. I had to have a double mastectomy. Do you know what that is? I lost both of my breasts. My husband left me and went to live with a much younger woman who worked at his company. I think they had been going together for some years."

My thoughts were, "He waited until the youngest son was a senior in high school and he would not have to pay much child support."

Angie continued, "As soon as I recovered, I hired a lawyer and immediately filed for divorce. The judge was kind to me and threw the book at my husband. I got the five-bedroom house in Porter Ranch that I'm living in, and the mortgage is paid. I got one-half of his profit-sharing account, one-half of his retirement benefits, one-half of his 401K. He was a top executive at his company."

I noticed for the first time; she was wearing all pink, a pink baseball cap, a pink top, pink pants, and pink sandals. I am not sure if she had a pink purse. The color pink is worn to honor breast cancer survivors during October, Breast Cancer Awareness Month. Angie still was an attractive woman, which she looked healthy.

As we rode along, she said, "I rent out two of the bedrooms to make a little extra money. My tenants are nurses; they both work at night. They are quiet, and they pay on time. I am a nurse, but I am not working right now.

"Shortly after the divorce was final, my husband came crying to me. He had been diagnosed with colon cancer, and he needed a colostomy. He asked me to forgive him, take him back and take care of him. I said, 'No, no, you will have to go to rehab or a nursing home.'"

His beautiful, young girlfriend had left him, and when he went to a nursing home, he fell and broke his hip. Having complications from the fall, he died a short time later.

"My house is now worth a lot of money. I am making it just fine."

From all outward appearances, Angie has moved on with her life.

"Til death do us part."

CHAPTER 18

I Want to Get Off Welfare.
I Want to Work

CARMEN

In the 1960s and 1970s, banking was different than it is today. Almost everyone received a paper paycheck. All transactions were pretty much done manually, as computers were not widely used. The bank gave the customers little paper savings books to keep a record of their account. My husband's payday was on Thursdays, and mine was on Fridays. So, I went to the bank every Friday.

The bank lines were different, there were several tellers, and you chose the line you wanted to stand-in. After a while, you knew all the tellers, and you tried not to get in the slow teller's line.

When I first started going to my bank located in South Central Los Angeles, the majority of the customers were African Americans, and all the tellers were white. Today, there is one line, and you go to the next available teller when your turn comes.

I got to know other customers who banked there. We always recognized and greeted each other. While going to the bank, I became friendly with an enthusiastic long-distance truck driver, who told me stories of his travels. He loved driving, and whenever possible, he took his family with him on some of his trips.

During this time, people on welfare received their checks on the first and fifteenth of every month, and they would do their banking on those days. The bank would be crowded, and the lines would go outside the door. There were two other banks in my area; however, the same situation was happening in those banks. Most working-class people would avoid going to the bank those days.

As I stood in line at the bank, one day, a well-dressed woman started a conversation with me. "See that Black woman sitting over there at the desk?"

"Yes."

"I knew her before she got that job, her name is Carmen."

I had noticed Carmen, too, when she started working at the bank. Whenever I frequently go to a place, I always remember people by sight, if not names, like in the workplace, church, or grocery store.

The lady went on to say, "One day, we were all standing in line to cash our checks when Carmen yelled at the banker, 'You need to hire some more people to work in here.'" She said Carmen was wearing a "Muumuu dress" (a loose dress of Hawaiian origin that hangs from the shoulder and is like a cross between a shirt and a robe) which was popular at the time, old house shoes, her hair was standing up on her head, and she was a hot mess. The manager went over to her and asked her, 'Do you want to work?' Carmen replied, "Yes, I want to work, I am tired of being on the welfare, but I don't have any training." The manager invited her over to his desk and made a few telephone calls. When Carmen left, he gave her a business card. After that, I didn't see Carmen in here for a while, the next time I saw Carmen, she was working as a teller. She had gone downtown Los Angeles and trained to work in here."

I remembered Carmen when she first started working in the bank. Her hair and skin were very oily, and she didn't wear any make-up. I am sure she did her own hair. The lady now sitting at the desk had a little resemblance to the lady who started as a teller. She was wearing a business suit, make-up, and her hair was neatly done.

I remember one day her sweater was very winkled. I felt bad for her, thinking she probably could not afford a decent sweater. When jobs became available to African Americans, many of us wanted our people to succeed and were happy to see other African Americans working in the business sector. We wanted our people to succeed and look good on the job.

What Carmen had going for herself was she was efficient and a fast learner. Many customers knew her by name and would get into her line even if there was a shorter line. She was well liked and respected, and had a quiet nature, and an appearance of humility about herself.

Over time, Carmen's appearance improved. One day, while in the bank, I saw her being trained in the safe deposit boxes/vault department. Shortly afterward, Carmen had a position sitting at a desk in the business section.

The lady continued with another story. I would never have thought she was a welfare recipient by looking at her. Her hair was well-groomed as if she went to the beauty salon, and I could tell it was tinted. She was clean, impeccably dressed, and pretty.

She went on to say, "I was standing right behind Carmen when the manager asked her if she wanted to work; I could have said yes, I want to work, but I didn't. I don't know why I was scared to say that I wanted to work. I have another long-time friend; someone told both of us they were hiring people down where they can fish. My friend went down and got hired. It took her a while, but she got a car. Now, she can buy her and her children a small house. She is no longer on welfare. I am still on welfare. When I told my boyfriend I wanted to go to work, canning fish, he told me he didn't want me coming home smelling like fish."

At the time, I was still relatively young and inexperienced in life. Therefore, I did not comment or reply to her situation about what I thought was a missed opportunity.

Today, I could give her lots of advice because of my life experiences and education. I would tell her to be her own person and stop thinking about what others think of her, especially the "boyfriend." If he wants her smelling good, he should provide for her. I would direct her to various schools, skill centers, and the like. Our County has "Upward Bound" programs to assist the financially challenged to get off welfare and become more independent.

I often think of her and wonder what happened to her when her children finally grew up, and she can no longer collect welfare. What happened to the boyfriend? What happens when her beauty fades? I wonder if her children become part of the welfare cycle.

SECTION 4
MISSION ACCOMPLISHED

CHAPTER 19
My Travels

Me at Niagara Falls

I was fascinated by the places I read about in my geography and history classes from a very early age. My father would bring copies of LIFE Magazine home from customers where he had painted. My older sister and I would look at these magazines together and fantasize about what we saw. So, even though my interest was always nursing, geography and history were my favorite subjects in school.

I didn't know how I would achieve my dream of seeing all the places I wanted to travel to, but I still had my hopes. Some places I had on my list were Paris, Israel, Hawaii, Rome, Hong Kong, Alaska, Africa, and the Caribbean Islands.

Fortunately, I traveled to Israel and Rome during the Lenten Season, where I witnessed a Jewish Passover Celebration which was very impressive. In addition, I saw and visited so many places I had read about in the Bible.

Hong Kong sparked my interest because several co-workers had gone there and told me about the beautiful silk material and gorgeous pearls you could buy. Plus, I had seen the movie "The World of Susan Wong," which fascinated me.

I regret that I didn't make it to Africa, my motherland. However, I have been told once a person of African descent step foot onto African soil; they are overcome with emotions and feel like they belong in Africa. Friends and family who have traveled to Africa have told me so much about their adventures.

Fortunately, I have traveled to many cities and states in the United States. The benefits of traveling are endless; to me, the most important benefit is that it educates the traveler. The traveler gets a chance to step back into history. For example, when I visited Alaska, I saw its first railroad and learned about the history of its buildings and surrounding communities.

Traveling allows one to experience how other people live in different parts of the world. On my trip to Israel, I was surprised to learn that glass existed before Christ was born. Glass making is believed to date from at least 2500 BC. In Israel, I saw pottery and other household items that archeologists had recently unearthed. It was so interesting to see columns brought from Africa to Israel before Christ was born, as Rome was in its glory days at this time. These columns are just lying on the ground near the amphitheater.

How did workers living at that time transport such large and heavy materials?

As mentioned, many modern day stadiums and churches are still being patterned after the ancient amphitheater. However, after many years and disasters, these structures are still standing. It's wonderful that people can visit these historical landmarks, buildings, and monuments.

Traveling allows one to see the strength and intellect of ancient human beings. But, I often wonder, how did ancient people build the pyramids in Egypt? How did the people build the Coliseum in Rome? What were their ethnicity and culture?

Through traveling, we can touch and walk on history and see what we have read about and watched on TV and in movies. I never dreamed that I would stand on the ground where King David tended his father's sheep. This space inspires the most quoted Psalm in the Bible, the 23rd Psalm. I have touched and prayed at the Wailing Wall in Jerusalem, caught water from the Jordan River, and brought it home with me. I visited many Holy sites in Israel. I walked in the Palm Sunday procession and was interviewed by a CNN reporter about whether I was afraid to be in Israel at that time. I wondered how he picked me out of such a vast crowd. When I was in Israel, I visited Bethlehem, the birthplace of Jesus the Christ, walked the ritual around the Church of the Holy Sepulcher, Jesus Christ's burial place, and received Holy Communion in Israel.

On my visit to Rome, I visited the famous Sistine Chapel and had an opportunity to see an incredible amount of some of the finest art in the world. There was so much to see that I didn't know where to look. I saw the works of the genius Michelangelo and purchased a book with many paintings I wanted to remember.

In Rome, I was a part of a large audience with Pope John Paul II; it was my second audience with Pope John Paul II. My first was when he visited Los Angeles, California, in 1987. Each audience was equally remarkable. I was close enough to reach out and touch him in Rome; however, I knew better; the Swiss guards surrounded the Pope.

I've heard many people say they don't like to travel. Some reasons are they're afraid to fly, there is too much water in the ocean, and they can't drink that much water; the distance is too great, and on and on. My husband told me he did enough traveling when he went overseas in the military. He would go on short trips or visits to his family, but he never would get on a ship again. Finally, after many years, I convinced him to go on a short cruise. Once he found out about the activities on a cruise ship, he was hooked.

I would never have thought I, a person from Eatonton, Georgia, would be financially able to take a weekend trip to New York, New York, to see "The Color Purple" on Broadway, written by Alice Walker, who is from Eatonton.

The earth is such a fascinating place. To view the earth from an airplane or a helicopter is transformative. To fly from one time zone to another is simply incredible to me. One minute it is nighttime; the next minute, it is daytime. Seeing a beautiful sunset from a place you're not from is unforgettable. The passengers described the recent trips to space as unreal and desired to go again. One of the most memorable places I have visited is Niagara Falls. I think it's one of God's most awesome creations.

I've been blessed to have seen so much but so little.

ABOUT THE AUTHOR

Frances Lowe is a native of Eatonton, Georgia, and migrated to Los Angeles, California, in 1961, looking for better educational and economic opportunities. She first began writing for a brief time at the urging of a nephew but abandoned her writing for several years.

Frances had a brief career with the Department of Defense but returned to school to pursue her lifelong dream to become a Registered Nurse. She dedicated twenty-seven years of her life to nursing. As a Registered Nurse at the Veteran's Hospital, Frances developed a booklet, *Daily Foot Care For the Diabetic Patient*, which is issued to diabetic patients.

In 2017, at a family reunion in her hometown, Frances and her younger sister, Sarah, came up with the idea of giving each child a $25.00 gift card for school supplies. This project has been successful. First, they identified thirty-eight children from pre-school to 18 years of age. Then next, they developed the Robert and Elizabeth Gorley Golden Handshake Award. It is a monetary award for high school graduates; if they are accepted to college, they will receive a higher amount. To date, four students have been accepted into an accredited college. One pre-med, cinema, international retail buyer, and Biomedical-science major. A portion of the profits from *Sunburst* will go to support the Robert and Elizabeth Gorley Golden Handshake Award.

Frances has been highly active in many organizations and her church and served on many committees. She was chairperson of her sorority scholarship ball for two years and made a profit each year. She chaired several fish fries at her church parish to benefit a school in Uganda, Africa. Frances was crowned queen of the senior citizen's community center cotillion, their primary annual fundraiser. In addition, Frances has cooked and served at several homeless shelters.

Over the years, Frances has had several hobbies. Before the 1994 Northridge Earthquake, Frances collected elephants, many from around the world. She has a large "tiny spoon" collection, again many from around the world. Many were gifts brought from family and friends' travel adventures. Today, Frances enjoys taking care of her extensive collection of house plants.

In the past, Frances was an above-average bowler, however, she won numerous trophies and awards at bowling. Frances loves nature; she enjoys looking at God's creation, water, trees, rocks, flowers, animals, birds, butterflies, and everything else. Frances loves to travel and see everything the planet earth has to offer. She loves meeting people of diverse cultures and different food of all cultures. Frances loves life.

She has been married to Marcus Lowe for fifty-plus years and is the mother of two children, Gregory and Melody and grandmother of six, and the great-grandmother of two. Frances resides in Southern California.

I have never regretted choosing nursing as my career.
—FRANCES LOWE, RN

A PSALM OF LIFE

Henry Wadsworth Longfellow
Beloved Poem of Mrs. Elizabeth Gorley

Tell me not, in mournful numbers,
Life is but an empty dream!
For the soul is dead that slumbers,
and things are not what they seem.

Life is real! Life is earnest!
And the grave is not it's goal.
Dust thou are, to dust returnest,
Was not spoken of the soul.

Not enjoyment, and not sorrow,
Is our destined end of way,
But to act, that each tomorrow
Find us farther, than today.

Art is long, and time is fleeting,
And our hearts, though stout and brave,
Still, like muffled drums are beating
Funeral marches to the grave.

In the world's broad field of battle,
In the bivouac of Life
Be not like dumb, driven cattle!
Be a hero in the strife!

SUNBURST

Trust no Future, how're pleasant!
Let the dead Past bury it's dead!
Act, -act in the living Present!
Heart within, and God o'erhead!

Lives of great men all remind us
We can make our lives sublime,
And, departing, leave behind us
Footprints on the sands of time:

Footprints, that perhaps another, Sailing o'er life solemn main,
A forlorn and shipwrecked brother, Seeing, shall take heart again

Let us, then be up and doing, with a heart for any fate;
Still achieving, still pursuing, learn to labor and to wait.

ACKNOWLEDGMENTS

Sarah Gorley Abrams
Bobby Baines
Delia Chambers
Ida Cochrane
Ruth Cross
Aliyah De Vivero
Melody Lowe De Vivero
De Andrea Freeman
David Granadino
James Anthony Gorley
Marilyn Holley

Ezekiel Joubert III
Sheri Kuppers
Barbara Perkins
Willie Jeff Reid
Mahogany Rose
Janie Taylor
Pamela Tiller
Leila J. Gorley Williams
Sophia Goode Williams
The Eatonton Messenger

Made in the USA
Columbia, SC
22 November 2022

71444571R00091